HERITAGE UNLOCKED
Guide to free sites in Cornwall and the Isles of Scilly

Cromwell's Castle, Tresco, Isles of Scilly

CONTENTS

As well as their many nationally renowned attractions, such as Tintagel Castle and Chysauster Ancient Village, Cornwall and the Isles of Scilly are home to many other ancient monuments to which entry is free. This guidebook provides a concise but informative introduction to each of these sites. The monuments range from prehistoric burial mounds to the extensive post-medieval defences of the Isles of Scilly, some of which saw service as recently as the Second World War.

The landscapes in this region are as changeable as the weather and as dramatic, with rugged granite geology softened only by the effects of a relatively mild climate. This land has been shaped by the sea and its people have long been part of a cultural exchange across the water. Communities have lived on the Isles of Scilly for thousands of years and the islands have played a major role in the nation's defences, as their many forts testify. In Cornwall, too, the sea is never far away, but its mineral wealth has had an equally powerful influence on the landscape. Today the physical legacy of many centuries of mining can be seen alongside monuments as varied as The Hurlers prehistoric stone circles and Penhallam medieval manor house.

Throughout this book, special features explore particular aspects of the region's history and character; the Cornish people's identity, for example, and the myths and legends that live on in this remote south-west peninsula. This book aims to encourage visitors to explore, understand and enjoy some of the lesser-known but no less intriguing monuments in English Heritage's care. A brief guide to English Heritage's paying sites is given at the end of the book.

Stone-slab footbridge over a Cornish stream

CORNWALL

The relative isolation of this far south-west peninsula has lent it an enduring mystery. It is a land of legend, with spectacularly located Tintagel Castle being a focus for stories of King Arthur for many centuries. Cornwall's isolation has also contributed to the impressive survival of its prehistoric monuments: monuments to the living and the dead,

such as Carn Euny ancient village and the burial chamber at Tregiffian. Cornwall's later history is rich and varied too, ranging from the inscribed 9th-century King Doniert's Stone to St Catherine's Castle, built in the 16th century to defend Fowey Harbour.

Cape Cornwall, West Penwith, Cornwall

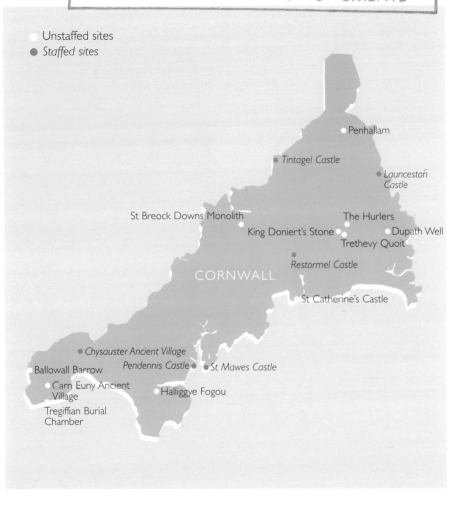

○ Unstaffed sites
● *Staffed sites*

Penhallam

● *Tintagel Castle*

● *Launceston Castle*

St Breock Downs Monolith

The Hurlers

King Doniert's Stone ○ Dupath Well

Trethevy Quoit

CORNWALL

● *Restormel Castle*

St Catherine's Castle

● *Chysauster Ancient Village*

Ballowall Barrow *Pendennis Castle* ● *St Mawes Castle*

○ Carn Euny Ancient Village

Halliggye Fogou

Tregiffian Burial Chamber

5

Cornwall's landscape bears the signs of centuries of excavation for its mineral wealth. Tin streaming has taken place on an industrial scale since medieval times and more evident still is the legacy of two centuries of deep-shaft mining that put Cornwall at the forefront of the Industrial Revolution.

Right: House A at Carn Euny Ancient Village

Opposite: The Hurlers stone circles, Bodmin Moor

Below: Herringbone slate wall west of Porthcothan, Cornwall

Cornwall has two cultural traditions. One results from a long association with the English and an administrative location as an English county, and from this standpoint people will happily define themselves as both Cornish and English. The other looks outwards for its inspiration to other Celtic countries and to the Cornish diaspora in the Americas and the Antipodes, created by a wave of emigration in the late 19th century. From within this tradition, the management of the Cornish heritage by a body called English Heritage can be seen as an effect of Cornwall's long history as England's first colony. Several

streams converge to make up this paradoxical identity. Among these are the echoes of the days before the 10th century when

Engineer Richard Trevithick, painted in 1816 by John Linnell

Cornwall was a British kingdom with its own rulers. Memories of independence underpin a persistently independent spirit, one that spurs many people to make an annual pilgrimage to St Keverne, home of Michael Angove, the blacksmith who led an army in 1497 to the gates of London. Risings like Angove's in the Tudor period can be linked back to medieval systems of government that occupied an ambiguous position in Cornwall, notably the Duchy of Cornwall, which was established in 1337, and the Stannary courts, set up in the 12th century to oversee the Cornish tin-mining industry.

The placenames of Cornwall remind us that its people spoke a British language, which persisted, even prospered, in mid and west Cornwall until the Reformation in the 16th century. And Cornish men and women looked to Breton, Welsh and native saints to maintain their sense of difference. Within this culture identity was strongly linked to landscape: for example, Cornish people were prone to take their second name from places, a practice that has left us that distinctive stock of Cornish surnames that begin with Tre, Pol or Pen.

It was perhaps a desire to link himself to popular memories of native rulers and places associated with Arthurian legends that led Earl Richard to build Tintagel Castle in the 1230s: a grandiose statement of power but a military folly.

Cornwall's industrial past plays its part too. With the quickening of the pulse of mining in the 1700s Cornwall became a 'landscape of fire', as steam engines helped drain the mines and draw up both men and ore from the depths. Now, the houses that contained those engines remain as stark reminders of the Industrial Revolution. As Cornish engineers such as Richard Trevithick busied themselves improving the steam engine to new heights of efficiency, the Cornish people were engaged in another revolution: a religious one. A visible icon of

this aspect of their identity is the small Methodist chapel tucked away in the Cornish countryside. Built by mining, fishing and farming communities, these chapels were a statement of their commitment to the message spread by John Wesley and his followers.

When Cornwall's mining economy faltered after the 1860s, de-industrialisation stimulated a new wave of emigration, and a new Cornwall was built in the later 1800s on far-off mining frontiers. For a time a

Above: The Seine Boat, *1904, by Newlyn School artist Alexander Stanhope Forbes*

Left: *Plain an Gwary at St Just, West Penwith*

transnational identity flourished, with flows of people, news and money connecting Cornwall to places across the globe.

Another strand in the paradox is the 'Celtic'. From the late 19th century Newlyn and St Ives artists began to represent the Cornish as primitive foils to urban 'civilisation', prompting other romantics to look to Cornwall's Celtic roots for their inspiration. The Celtic 'revival' began in the early years of the 1900s. This movement looked back to the Cornish language and to Cornwall's Celtic connections to restore a sense of pride in the midst of a shattered industrial landscape. Over the course of the 20th century this blossomed, restoring Cornwall's 'Celtic' past and linking it to aspects of contemporary culture, such as music, dance and even surfing. Other parts of Cornwall's landscape were now emphasised, for example the Plain an Gwarys, like Perran Round, where medieval Cornish miracle plays had been performed; or the Oratory of St Piran, patron saint of Cornish tinners. Half-buried in the sands at Perranporth, this is now the site of an annual re-enactment of Piran's story and a place of pilgrimage for visitors from all over the world.

The Cornish identity is thus a heady and changing blend of rebelliousness, language, industrialisation and Celtic revival. To this mixture is now added a reinvigorated Cornish transnationalism as people of Cornish descent overseas rediscover their roots. The result is a modern identity that connects to California, Australia or Brittany as well as eastwards across the River Tamar to England and one that uses its rich heritage to generate hopes for the future.

Left: *St Piran's Oratory*

Opposite: *Cheesewrings Quarry, Bodmin Moor*

View from the site of Ballowall Barrow

This large, chambered mound, or cairn, is one of the most complex and impressive burial monuments to survive from the Bronze Age (*c* 2500–750 BC). It lies right on the coast near Land's End, with marvellous views from Cape Cornwall to Sennen and even to the Isles of Scilly on a clear day. Also known as

Carn Gluze (or Gloose) – the Cornish for grey rock – the cairn was excavated in 1878–9, after it had long lain buried under the spoil heaps of neighbouring mines.

A number of prehistoric funerary cairns of similar date are sited prominently along the western coast of Penwith, at the western tip of

Cornwall, an area which is also rich in other types of prehistoric monuments including settlement sites and field systems. Ballowall, however, is unique in its size and complexity. What exists today is the result of a number of stages of construction, the sequence of which is not easy to unravel. Radically altered over several centuries of use, the barrow eventually enshrined several different types of burial monument, and must have been as resonant of the beliefs of earlier generations as a medieval parish church is today.

Visitors to the site first see a wide platform of heaped rubble and earth, within which is a circular trench surrounding the stump of a central mound. At the centre of the mound is a large oblong cavity containing a T-shaped pit. The trench and cavity are not part of the original design of the barrow: they were dug out by a gang of local miners for William Copeland Borlase, who excavated Ballowall in the late 19th century and left his trenches open and revetted

in order to present the monument to visitors. These unfilled archaeological trenches obscure the earlier appearance of the barrow, making it harder to appreciate its original form.

The cairn's central mound is a truncated dome up to 35 ft (10.7m) across and 8 ft (2.5m) high. Surrounding it, and added at a later date, is the wide, near-circular platform, nearly 78 ft (24m) in diameter. It was originally about 5 ft (1.5m) high but some of the rubble

The 'viewing trenches' left by William Copeland Borlase

The sea-facing burial chamber, the earliest part of the barrow

from the 19th-century excavations was heaped onto it, producing its present irregular surface and increasing its height to up to 8ft (2.5m). Records from Borlase's excavations reveal that, in its final prehistoric form, the central mound was defined by two drystone walls, one abutting the inner edge of the platform. The outer edge of the platform is defined by a steep drystone wall above a kerb of large slabs.

The earliest part of the barrow is a rectangular burial chamber, now under the outer wall of the platform, facing the sea. The chamber is about 10 ft (3m) long by 3 ft (1m) wide and is capped by stone slabs. It seems to have been a typical entrance grave, a type of tomb usually associated with the Isles of Scilly, where many similar monuments are found. On the mainland they are concentrated in Penwith, at the western tip of Cornwall, another example being Tregiffian Burial Chamber. The entrance grave at Ballowall could predate the main structure of the cairn by several centuries. Usually such entrance graves were covered by a roughly circular mound, which must here have been incorporated in the later platform.

When the grave was excavated, pieces of prehistoric pottery and cremated bone were found in the chamber floor. Within the mound and platform the excavators also found the remains of three pits, perhaps for burials or for some other ritual purpose, and seven funerary cists – small, stone-lined, box-like structures. Two of the pits, which originally adjoined the entrance grave, are now visible as the T-shape within the cairn's central cavity. A third large, oval pit can be seen on the south-east side of the cairn.

Four of the funerary cists were discovered near the T-shaped pit under the central mound, and two of them contained small funerary urns. Another cist, containing pottery dating to the Bronze Age, was found high up in the rubble of the mound. Two others were found beneath the platform and must therefore post-date the central mound. Both of these later cists are visible in the floor of Borlase's trench.

At the end of its long period of use as a burial place, Ballowall must have appeared as a tall dome of stone projecting upwards from a steep-sided, flat-topped platform. The various earlier monuments concealed within this imposing structure would not have been visible, but would have been known to the communities that would have linked them together into a statement of identity and status. Platform cairns, cists and ritual pits, though rare, are widely distributed across England; the combination here of all of these, together with an entrance grave, makes Ballowall unique and helps to shed light on the diversity of burial practices and social organisation among prehistoric communities.

Borlase's trenches can be seen clearly from the air

On the cliff edge 1 mile W of St Just, nr Carn Gloose *OS Map 203; ref SW 355312*

Above: One of the Iron Age hut circles: House 1

Right: The ancient hut circles of Carn Euny

Carn Euny is one of the best preserved ancient villages in south-west England, where visitors can explore the remains of individual stone houses, some of a type unique to Cornwall. The village was occupied from the Iron Age until about the end of the Roman occupation of Britain (*c* 750 BC–AD 400) and has an excellent example of an underground stone-walled passage known as a fogou (the late-Cornish word for a cave).

Carn Euny lies on a south-west slope on granite uplands rich in antiquities. The hill above it to the north-east is crowned by the circular Iron Age fort of Caer Bran, and immediately above the village to the north-west on the Bartinney Downs are the remains of earlier Bronze Age settlement sites and field systems.

The village was first discovered by tin miners in the early 19th century, but it was not extensively excavated until 1964–72. It has suffered damage over the years from stone-robbing and farming and the overall layout is not easy to make out. There seem to have been at least 10 houses belonging to several different periods of occupation, from the Iron Age onwards. The houses cluster together

in a haphazard interlocking pattern, often sharing walls. In contrast, Chysauster Iron Age village has a regular street pattern.

All the stone houses visible today at Carn Euny were built during the Romano-British period, between the 2nd and 4th centuries AD. Many of the walls remain up to 3 ft (1m) high. The houses are of two types. Seven, including a row of four to the south (on the left after the modern entrance), are simple, single-roomed, round or oval houses – the standard house type across Cornwall at the time. The remains of an earlier, timber-built Iron Age round house were found in this area during excavation and there must have been other similar houses here during the Iron Age, which were subsequently replaced by the stone houses visible today.

The three remaining excavated houses, adjoining each other along the south-east side of the fogou, are of the type known as 'courtyard houses', so called because they contain a number of rooms opening off a central courtyard. This style seems to be typical of the houses on the Land's End peninsula and was perhaps an adaptation to the wind- and rainswept local conditions.

The courtyard houses are all similar in plan and are built on a much larger scale than the simple round houses. They are enclosed by an immensely thick outer wall, faced inside and out with drystone masonry. A paved entrance, facing away from the prevailing south-west wind, leads into the courtyard, off which open a number of small rooms built into the thickness of the enclosing wall. These may have been sleeping places or workshops. A large oval or circular room opposite the entrance was probably the main living room, and one or more long narrow rooms on either side of the courtyard would have been used for storage and stabling. Stone-covered drainage gullies, to carry water in and out, can be seen in the floors.

Inside the fogou

Thatch roofing is thought to have covered the rooms and possibly the courtyard as well.

Carn Euny also boasts a fogou, a complex of underground tunnels of a kind almost entirely restricted to the far west of Cornwall. These mysterious structures typically have a main stone-lined passage, often with narrow side passages known as creeps. Most were built during the later Iron Age (*c* 400 BC–AD 43). The fogou at Carn Euny has a sloping, unroofed entrance at the east end (probably a late addition), a long,

curving main passage roofed with 11 capstones, and a creep at the southern end that leads up to the surface. What makes it unique among fogous is that it also has a round chamber, 15 ft (4.6m) across, which seems to have been built in the 5th century BC, so predating the rest of the fogou. This chamber now lies beneath one of the later round houses.

The purpose of fogous has been the subject of much debate, and excavations have cast little light. One theory is that they may have been hideouts in times of trouble; another

Facing page: This reconstruction of Chysauster Ancient Village gives an idea of how Carn Euny might have looked in the Iron Age

Right: Plan of the fogou

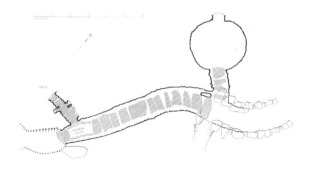

18

is that they were used as cellars for storing goods or livestock. It has also been suggested that fogous might have had some sort of ritual significance. On the west side of the site there is a small rectangular cottage, which was occupied in the last half of the 18th century. By the mid-19th century it had already been abandoned. It may have been built over the remains of another courtyard house.

The layout of the houses and excavations here and elsewhere provide much evidence for the villagers' way of life. It has been suggested that a typical courtyard house might have been home to an extended family group, giving a population of about 60 for the known extent of the later settlement at Carn Euny. The villagers seem to have practised mixed farming, growing cereals and keeping sheep, goats and perhaps cattle in the fields around the village; and they may have traded in tin, streamed in the valley below. Tools found during excavation show that weaving, grinding corn and other

domestic industries were all carried out here. The basic pattern of existence at Carn Euny seems to have changed very little over the long period in which the village was in use – life in the far west of Cornwall was apparently little affected by the Roman occupation. The village appears to have been abandoned peacefully, but we do not know why.

Chysauster Ancient Village, also in the care of English Heritage, is well worth a visit, as is Halangy Down on St Mary's, Isles of Scilly; and one of the best preserved fogous is at Halliggye on the Lizard peninsula.

1¼ miles SW of Sancreed off A30; 660yd (600m) walk from car park in Brane
OS Map 203; ref SW 402288

Without a doubt, the founding father of Cornish archaeology was Dr William Borlase. Born near St Just in 1696, into an old and wealthy local family, Borlase was intrigued from an early age by almost everything he encountered and became a tireless correspondent with scientists, naturalists and antiquarians far from his native Cornwall. He travelled widely around Cornwall well-equipped with notebooks – most of which survive – and his major

Above: William Borlase began his archaeological observations at an early age

Opposite: Ink drawing of a house at Pendeen, St Just, in William Borlase's unpublished Excursions 1751–58

publications, including *Observations on the Antiquities … of the County of Cornwall* (1754) and *Observations on the Ancient and Present State of the Isles of Scilly* (1756), quickly established him as a scholar of national renown. Some of Borlase's views, on the Phoenician and Danish influence on Cornwall's past, for example, find no support today. But set against what he did – effectively create an archaeological interest in his beloved Cornwall – this hardly matters. He sought out, measured and drew countless sites and objects and in his week-long trip to the Isles of Scilly he deduced the post-Roman submergence, by rising sea-levels, that had created these islands in a way that would only be fully described two centuries later. In 1753, anticipating 20th-century schemes of recording everything on a parish basis, Borlase sent every Cornish incumbent a questionnaire about antiquities in their parishes; shamefully he only had eight replies. His promotion of purposeful fieldwork was a vital contribution to the developing field of archaeology.

Borlase's great-great-grandson, William Copeland Borlase, was born in 1848.

He rapidly exhibited the same interests as his ancestor and excavated the underground passage, or fogou, at Chapel Euny near Sancreed at the age of just 15. In 1878 he conducted his most spectacular excavation, the great cliff-edge prehistoric cairn at Ballowall, St Just. His first book, *Naenia Cornubia*, was published the same year: a detailed account of mostly Neolithic and Bronze Age burial sites. His 1878 *The Age of the Saints* was a pioneer study of early Christian Cornwall. W Copeland Borlase had a distinguished public career – he was an MP for East Cornwall in 1880 – but in 1887 a vindictive Portuguese former mistress brought about his moral exposure and bankruptcy. He lost his parliamentary seat, and the Borlase family library and

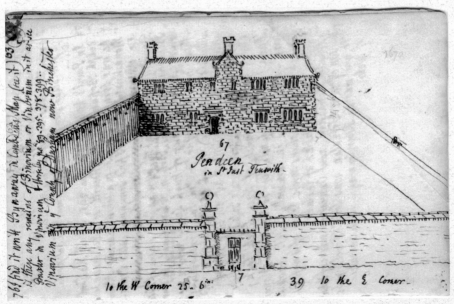

archaeological collections had to be auctioned. Borlase went abroad, shunned by his relatives and cut off from Cornwall, and died in 1889 aged only 41.

John Thomas Blight was born in 1835. He was also a Cornishman, but did not have the material advantages of the Borlase family.

John Thomas Blight

Encouraged by his father, self-taught, observant and talented, the young Blight came to know the Land's End district and much of west Cornwall as few have done then or since. He was a fine artist, producing his own wood engravings and illustrating his numerous articles and books. His 1861 work, *A Week at the Land's End,* a detailed archaeological ramble and probably his finest book, was followed in 1865 by *Churches of West Cornwall.* Blight's interests were, archaeologically, as wide as these titles suggest. But again, all this was to end in tragedy. By 1871 it was clear that he was hopelessly insane and he was committed to the County Lunatic Asylum at Bodmin. Out of the public eye Blight was progressively forgotten and in 1884 several printed sources declared that he had died. The truth was hardly less sad; he lingered on, oblivious to the world outside, until January 1911. His books, though, were reissued and continue to be cited. Blight brought a multi-period approach to the archaeology of Cornwall – he was as concerned to record an 18th-century ruined house as a chambered cairn of *c* 1800 BC – and, like the Borlases, his meticulous accuracy in recording set new standards for Cornish archaeology in the 19th century.

S.W. View

J.T. BLIGHT

Bosphrennis Beehive hut.

Frederick Christian Hirst was born in India in 1874 and educated in England. After a career in the army, during which he had served as Director of Surveys for Bengal and Assam and published works on early mapping and boundaries, he retired to a rented cottage at Zennor in 1924. A stocky, moustachioed chain-smoker, usually seen in tweed hat and plus-fours, Fred Hirst revolutionised Cornish archaeology. Nobody else in Cornwall at that time was familiar with contemporary European ideas about prehistory or with systematic methods of excavation. After a brief spell directing excavations, Hirst and a band of close friends founded the West Cornwall Field Club in 1935. As its president, he continued excavations at the large, Roman-period, native settlement at Porthmeor, similar to those at Chysauster and Carn Euny. Hirst also began a museum of old agricultural and mining implements, which survives as the Wayside Folk Museum at Bridge Cottage, Zennor. The Field Club continued to be active after Hirst's death, and became the Cornwall Archaeological Society in 1961.

From Hirst's papers it is clear that he anticipated virtually every development in

Cornish and national archaeology. A network of parish correspondents and field monument wardens, training schemes, local authority liaison, rescue work, a proper archive and central reporting – it is all there.

Above: Fred Hirst taking a break from his excavations at Porthmeor in 1938

Left: An unpublished watercolour of Bosphrennis Beehive hut by J T Blight

23

Right: The front of the well-house with its bell turret

Below right: Detail of the well-house roof

The custom of venerating springs and wells has a long tradition, not only in Christianity but in the pre-Christian religions in Britain. Some Christian wells clearly had earlier origins as sacred sites. Cornwall alone has more than a hundred wells and springs which are believed to have healing waters. In the medieval period the cult of holy wells was very strong, and during that time about 40 Cornish springs or wells had structures of some kind built over them, usually simple gabled houses. Dupath is an unusually large and late example of such a holy well-house, and it has survived largely unaltered.

The small chapel-like building was probably built in about 1510 by the Augustinian canons of the nearby priory of St Germans, to whom the site belonged. The architecture of the well-house is typical of the late 15th and early 16th centuries. Built of Cornish granite, it has a steeply-pitched roof, built from courses of granite slabs that run the length of the building. There are badly weathered pinnacles at each corner and a small bell turret, with a highly elaborate

Facing page, left: The overflow to the holy spring

canopy, over the entrance. The interior is lit by one small vertical slit window in each side wall and a larger decorated window in the north-east wall.

The spring rises a little way in front of the building and flows under the entry threshold. Inside, it runs via a restored granite gutter into a sunken stone basin at the far end, which was presumably used for bathing. An overflow leads outside at the back into a medieval circular trough.

At one time the spring at Dupath was believed to cure whooping cough, and it has been suggested that, in addition to its role in healing the sick, the spring may have been used on occasion for baptisms. The little

building may have been a worthwhile financial investment for the canons of St Germans, since visitors to the spring would have left offerings, much as they do at wishing wells today. We know from monastic records that such sources of income were jealously guarded by religious houses.

Although the cult of holy wells was condemned at the time of the Reformation in the mid-16th century, local reverence for them and folklore customs continued, in some cases to the present day. They often attracted local legend: one grim tale associated with Dupath recounts that two Saxons – Colan (Cornish for heart or courage) and Gottlieb – fought a duel there for a lady's hand. But the maiden went unmarried: Colan was killed outright and Gottlieb fatally wounded, though some versions say he died later of 'impatience'.

The spring flowing under the threshold

1 mile E of Callington off A388 (Access is through a farmyard)
OS Map 201; ref SX 375692

The mysterious tunnel complexes known as fogous are almost entirely restricted to the far west of Cornwall, and Halliggye is the largest and one of the best preserved. Visitors can explore its atmospheric narrow passages, once part of an Iron Age settlement.

The fogou lies within a type of settlement known as a round. These were small enclosures defined by banks and a ditch, and would have contained small timber or stone houses, round or oval in plan, often set around the edge. Excavation has revealed that Halliggye was occupied from the 5th or 4th century BC, making it one of the earliest known examples of this kind of settlement. Traces survive of two curving concentric ramparts separated by a ditch: the steep face of the ramparts were probably faced with timber or stone and topped with a breastwork. The defences enclosed an area about 230 ft (70m) across. Nothing is known of the buildings inside.

The fogou lies in the north-west part of the round; the entrance, via modern steps, is along a short open passage with its original sloping floor. Apart from this section the passages of the fogou run entirely underground, and are walled with drystone rubble and roofed with huge flat slabs or capstones. The fogou contains several distinct sections, revealed by excavation in the 1980s to have been built at different times.

The fogou originally consisted of one straight passage, more than 30 ft (9m) long, which led from the round interior towards the rampart. Just before the north-west end of this main passage a doorway leads left into a long, curving side passage (low at first but soon increasing in height) that follows the line of the round's inner rampart for 60 ft (19m). At a later date, and perhaps to provide more security, two narrow passageways known as creeps were added. The northern one, at the end of the main passage, is 15 ft (4.5m) long and up to 3 ft (1m) high and ends in a doorway, now blocked, at the base of the round's ditch. The southern creep is only 9 ft (3m) long and opens off the southern end of the curved side passage. Creeps have been found at other fogous; in this case they seem to have been added at about the time of the Roman invasion of Britain (AD 43).

During the Roman period the defences of the round seem to have been dismantled; however, fragments of pottery from Roman north Africa found at the site indicate that by the 5th century AD it was the home of a local nobleman.

The purpose of fogous remains an enigma. They are all associated with some kind of settlement – either rounds, as here, or hillforts, or within courtyard settlements, such as that at Carn Euny. All were in use during the Iron Age and Roman period. There is no lack of theories as to their function: safe refuges, storage areas, or ritual shrines have all been suggested. The addition of the creeps at Halliggye with their low, narrow entrances supports the idea that it might have provided a refuge at some point in its history. Excavation has revealed a great deal about the fogou, but much still remains a mystery.

Below left: Inside Halliggye Fogou

5 miles SE of Helston off B3293, E of Garras on Trelowarren Estate. Estate entry charged.
Open reasonable daylight hours Easter–Oct; closed Nov–Mar. A torch is essential.
OS Map 203; ref SW 713239

*Part of the central
circle of The Hurlers*

Some 150 prehistoric stone circles
have been identified in England, of
which 16 are to be found on Bodmin
Moor, the largest of the Cornish
granite uplands. Of these, The Hurlers
are the most fascinating. The close
grouping of three Late Neolithic or
Early Bronze Age stone circles is
extremely rare in England, but a
grouping of three such regular circles
is unique.

The circles form part of a moorland
landscape rich in prehistoric remains.
Detailed archaeological survey of
Bodmin Moor has yielded much
evidence of human exploitation from
earliest prehistoric times. In the Bronze
Age, as now, this part of Bodmin
Moor appears to have been an area of
upland grazing, overlooking cultivated
fields in the lower valleys.

The monument, which was
excavated in the 1930s, consists of
three adjacent stone circles aligned
north-east to south-west. To the west
is a pair of outlying upright stones
standing close together, known as the
Pipers. Of the northern circle 15
original stones are visible, and
excavation revealed the buried holes
for a further ten, now represented by
marker stones. The regular spacing of
the stones suggests there would have
been five more, giving 30 in all. A
strip of granite paving, found in
excavation, ran between this and the
central circle. The central circle, the
best preserved of the three, has 14
original stones and 14 markers. All

the stones were hammered smooth, and the chippings were deposited nearby. The southern circle, which has not been excavated, is the least well preserved: it has nine original stones of which seven have fallen.

Stone robbing has damaged all the circles to some extent, while the introduction of cattle on to Bodmin Moor has resulted in many of the stones falling over: cows use them as scratching posts, eroding the ground and undermining them. The small pits visible within the southern and central circles, and a slight bank crossing the central circle, are the remains of post-medieval tin mining.

The monument forms one element in an extensive grouping of later Neolithic and Bronze Age ceremonial and funerary monuments on this part of Bodmin Moor, and the circles are directly aligned with some of these. The axis through the centres of the two northern circles aligns directly on the massive Rillaton Barrow, visible on the skyline to the north-east, while the axis of the southern pair of

THE HURLERS.

circles in turn aligns directly with a prehistoric round cairn to the south-west. Another line at right angles to this axis through the central circle takes in another stone circle, an embanked avenue and a stone row. Such circles are likely to have had considerable ritual importance for the societies that used them.

For the best part of 4,000 years The Hurlers have kept their secrets. A local legend identifies The Hurlers as men who were turned to stone for playing the ancient game of hurling on a Sunday. The two isolated stones of the Pipers are said to be the figures of two men who played tunes on a Sunday and suffered the same fate.

In 1650 John Norden described the stones as like 'men performinge that pastime Hurlinge'

*½ mile NW
of Minions
off B3254;
signposted from
Common Moor
OS Map 201;
ref SX 258714*

Right: The 9th-century stone crosses; King Doniert's Stone is in the foreground

Facing page, left: John Norden's depiction of the stones in 1650

Facing page, right: The inscription bearing the name of the Cornish king

These two fragments, one of which is known as King Doniert's Stone, are the only surviving examples of 9th-century stone crosses in Cornwall. The inscription on King Doniert's Stone, bearing the name of a Cornish king, is the only such cross to feature a character known also from documentary sources.

Cornwall, like Ireland and Scotland, lay on the fringe of the Roman world, and there are few signs of Roman influence in the region.

The name the Romans used to denote this territory in the south-west was Dumnonia. Following the collapse of Roman rule at the beginning of the 5th century AD, much of eastern Britain fell under the control of Saxon invaders; however, Dumnonia, which included Devon and parts of Somerset as well as Cornwall, remained an independent kingdom for several centuries. Historical and archaeological evidence for this period is scant, but it was during this time that Christianity was first brought to Cornwall by Welsh and Irish monks. The early missionaries are thought to have set up wooden crosses to proclaim the victory of Christ in the places where they preached: in time these sites became sanctified, and stone crosses were erected in place of the older wooden ones.

King Doniert's Stone may be the base of one such cross and the taller broken shaft alongside it is probably another. King Doniert's Stone stands about 4 ft 6 in (1.37m) high, and is decorated on three of its faces with interlaced ornament of a style common throughout Britain. The upper end of the stone has a deep mortice in the top to take an upper shaft or cross head. The east face bears a weathered inscription which reads *Doniert rogavit pro anima* ('Doniert has asked [for this to be made] for his soul['s sake']). The clue to Doniert's identity lies in a passage in the early Welsh chronicle known as the *Annales Cambriae*, which names a king of Dumnonia called Dumgarth (or Dwingarth). He is recorded as having drowned in the sea in about AD 875.

The southern cross-shaft fragment is taller, about 7 ft (2.1m) high, and one face has a panel of interlaced decoration. Excavations have revealed an underground rock-cut passage that starts to the south-east of the crosses and terminates in a cross-shaped chamber beneath the two stones. The relationship between the underground chamber and the crosses has yet to be explained.

The stones appear in antiquary John Norden's *Description of Cornwall*.

I mile NW of St Cleer off B3254, between Redgate and Common Moor
OS Map 201; ref SX 236688

Cornwall derived its wealth from its geology. Its granite uplands extend westwards from Dartmoor to West Penwith, creating a spine of outcrops, each surrounded by a ring of rocks known locally as killas. Mineralisation here has created rich lodes, or deposits, of tin, copper, zinc, lead and iron.

This mineral wealth has been exploited since prehistoric times, giving Cornwall early importance as a supplier of metals to Britain and northern Europe. Tin was gathered at the surface or from streamworks – shallow excavations for ore redeposited in riverbeds. Fashioned oak from Pentewan tin streamworks has been radiocarbon dated to around 2190 BC, the Early Bronze Age. Surface tin was alloyed with copper to make bronze. Copper was obtained from shallow 'openworks', though Middle Bronze Age tools found in an opencast copper mine at Godolphin suggest that

deeper mining might also have been taking place at this time. Classical writer Diodorus Siculus refers to Iron Age tin trading at Ictis, a location claimed for St Michael's Mount in the west and Mount Batten in Plymouth, among others. Many Cornish valleys show evidence of medieval or later streamworks – activity which has obscured much of the evidence for prehistoric mining – whilst tin streaming continued into the early 20th century.

By the medieval period tin streaming was being undertaken on an industrial

scale. In the 12th century legal control of virtually every aspect of Cornwall's tin mining industry was granted to Richard, Earl of Cornwall and the Stannary system conceived; a Stannary being a tin mining district with its own administration. The principal towns in the Stannaries performed a role similar to modern customs' control.

From the late 17th century copper mines were, in many regions, of greater significance in terms of the sheer quantity of ore produced and their impact on the Cornish landscape and economy than were the tin mines. By the 19th century the greatest copper-mining district was around St Day and Gwennap, where the Consolidated and United Mines both produced nearly a million tons from 1815 to 1872. Copper was used in great amounts to sheathe the hulls of ships, in coinage and for electric cables, and in smaller amounts as a component of brass. When production slowed in the second half of the century and mines began to close, a few diversified into arsenic production. The Tamar Valley Mines alone at one time provided over half the world's arsenic supply.

Above: Section through a Cornish beam engine

Facing page and left: Bottallack mine in about 1860 and as it looks today

From the late 18th century iron foundries and engineering workshops were built and three of these – Harvey's, Copperhouse and Perran foundries – employed approximately 3,000 people at one time.

The need to pump water and haul ore and waste rock from ever deeper shafts led to the rapid development of steam and other technologies. As a result Cornwall produced many great engineers, among them Richard Trevithick who designed the world's first steam carriage. Engineers William West and Arthur Woolf greatly improved the Cornish beam steam engines, which had to pump from as much as 2,000 ft down in the 'hard rock' granite mines.

By the mid 19th century there were in excess of 2,000 mines and Cornish miners and their machinery played a crucial role in extending Britain's industrial revolution throughout the world. Harvey's Foundry made iron components for, and assembled and installed, Cornish beam steam engines in Australia, South Africa, South America and Spain (carried there by ships also built by the company).

Cornish innovation was not limited to mining technology, however, and the 19th century also saw the emergence of significant ancillary industries including the gunpowder industry, safety-fuse production, and the manufacture of rock drills and compressed-air equipment.

Cornwall during the late 18th and early 19th centuries was probably the most important centre of innovation and technological development in the country.

Tin continued to be produced in large quantities as copper production fell, but by the turn of the 19th century, with the main lodes exhausted, many of the mines had folded. From 1860 to 1890 many thousands of Cornish miners had to emigrate to use their only skill in alternative mining employment overseas.

Much of the infrastructure that was developed to maintain these massive undertakings is still present in the Cornish landscape – the mineral tramways, railways and roads, inclines and canals connecting the mines with the ports from which their products were exported. Many of the larger mine buildings such as engine and boiler houses remain, some preserved as ruins. Good examples include: the Botallack-Levant mines in West Penwith; Phoenix United-South Caradon mines at Minions, Liskeard; and Gunnislake Clitters-Okel Tor mines in the Tamar Valley. Scores of mining settlements survive across the county, their inhabitants now engaged in other industries but their architecture a lasting testament to the massive industrialisation of an earlier age. Cornwall and West Devon's bid for World Heritage Site status seeks to promote, protect and preserve the industrial archaeology of the south-west peninsula.

Facing page: A Cornish miner in the 19th century

Above: Bassett mines near Carnkie, Redruth

Right: Copyright label from Bickford Smith & Co, fuse manufacturers

Above: The low
ruins of Andrew de
Cardinham's moated
manor house

Facing page: The
various phases of
construction at
Penhallam

These low, grass-covered ruins are
the remains of a moated 13th-century
manor house built by Andrew de
Cardinham. Moated manor houses
are found mainly in central and
eastern England, but are rare in the
south-west. Penhallam is also unusual
because, having been abandoned in
the 14th century, its full medieval
ground plan has survived unaltered
by later building work.

The manor house was excavated
between 1968 and 1973. Some of the
original walls survive and elsewhere

the course of the foundations
recorded during excavation are
marked by low, turf-covered banks
that were built over their courses.

The de Cardinhams were a family
of minor barons who profited from
the favour of King John (reigned
1199–1216). John's determination to
recover Normandy, lost to the king of
France in 1204, meant that he spent
most of his reign trying to raise large
sums of money. Robert Fitzwilliam,
Lord of Cardinham, seems to have
become John's principal agent in

Cornwall, helping to exploit the justice system in the king's interest. His reward was an increase in status and possessions, and an enhanced inheritance for his son Andrew, who also held Restormel Castle.

Although Penhallam seems to have been built in various stages between the late 12th and early 14th centuries, Andrew de Cardinham is assumed to have been responsible for the main building phase, in the 1220s and 1230s. There are the remains of an earthwork castle at Week St Mary nearby, which could have been the first home of the family in the area. The building of Penhallam may represent a move to a more sheltered site, when the need for defence was no longer a primary consideration.

The house was built on an island surrounded by a flat-bottomed moat, up to 40 ft (12m) wide in places. This still contains water on three sides – the fourth has silted up. The siting of the castle at the floor of a deep valley required careful water

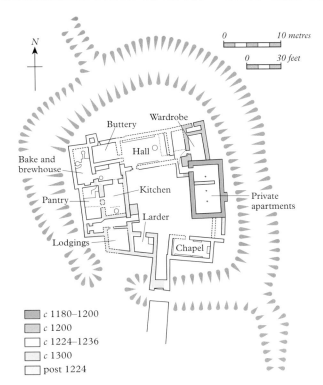

N

| | 0 | 10 metres |
| | 0 | 30 feet |

Buttery
Wardrobe
Hall
Bake and brewhouse
Kitchen
Pantry
Larder
Private apartments
Lodgings
Chapel

◼ c 1180–1200
◻ c 1200
☐ c 1224–1236
☐ c 1300
☐ post 1224

management to prevent periodic flooding and to control the flow of water into the moat. This was achieved by diverting the course of the larger of the two tributaries flowing along

37

Above: The inner courtyard as it might have looked in the 13th century

Facing page: The layout of the house can still be understood from the ruins

fixed bridge with stone abutments at either end. On the island a passageway led from the bridge to an impressive entrance tower in the south range of the manor house. This gave access to the inner courtyard around which the four ranges of the house were built.

Immediately to the right (east) of the entrance tower in the south range was a chapel: its stone benches and the base of an altar survive. In the east range, which seems to have been the first to be built, lay the owner's private apartments at first-floor level. At the northern end a wardrobe and garderobe (latrine) were added later – on the ground floor you can still see the line of the sewer that carried the waste from the garderobe to the moat, a healthier arrangement than in some medieval buildings.

The north range is dominated by the hall: the remains of the dais – the

the valley into an artificial channel at a higher level.

The house was built round a quadrangle and the original entrance was across a drawbridge on the south side, on the site of the modern bridge. The drawbridge was operated from an early-13th-century gatehouse on the edge of the island. Later in the century this arrangement was replaced by a

site of the high table – are still visible at its east end, as are the stone-faced benches lining the east, north and south walls. Doorways at the west end of the hall led into the buttery, from which wine and beers were served, and the servery (for serving food). Further west was a single-storey lean-to bakehouse, with a malting kiln at its north end.

The west range housed the kitchen, which seems to have been rebuilt in about 1300 – perhaps as a result of a fire – and a lean-to pantry. At the southern end of this range was a two-storey lodging for the household staff. The rubble-built garderobe that served both floors still projects west from the lodgings. The western half of the south range, between the lodgings and the entrance, contains a larder, which had a stone-lined cool-storage pit in its north-east corner.

Penhallam seems to have been lived in for a relatively short time. Andrew de Cardinham died in about 1256 without a male heir, and his lands were split equally between his

daughters. By 1270 Penhallam had descended through the female line to the Champernowne family, and by the early 14th century it had been passed to tenants. Partitioning of the manor's lands had begun by 1330 and was complete by 1428. Local people would then have helped themselves to the building materials, quickly reducing the deserted shell to its foundations.

For a long time the site was almost unknown, but the threat of tree planting led to its excavation between 1968 and 1973, when the ruins were consolidated and the outline of the walls restored. The site is now a peaceful nature reserve set within a wooded valley. The de Cardinham and Champernowne families feature in Daphne du Maurier's 1968 novel *The House on the Strand*.

1 mile NW of Week St Mary off minor road, off A39 from Treskinnick Cross (10-min walk from car park on forest track)
OS Map 190; ref SX 224974

The largest and heaviest monolith in Cornwall

surrounding countryside and across to the sea. It is the largest and heaviest monolith in Cornwall, weighing in at about 16.5 tons (16.75 tonnes), and probably dates to the Late Neolithic to mid-Bronze Age (*c* 2500–1500 BC).

Standing stones or monoliths are rare in England but are scattered across the country, with concentrations in Cornwall, the North Yorkshire Moors, Cumbria, Derbyshire and the Cotswolds. Their purpose remains a subject for speculation today. Their accompanying features show that they had a ritual function: they are among several types of monument of late-Neolithic or Bronze Age date that are often found, when excavated, to be associated with evidence of cremation. They may also have functioned as markers for routeways, territories, graves or meeting-points.

The monolith on St Breock Downs stands within a low stone mound or cairn, which measures about 33 ft (10m) across, and is formed from the local Devonian shale

This massive stone stands near the summit of the St Breock Downs, offering beautiful views of the

which has extensive feldspar veining. The stone itself is 16 ft (4.9m) long but it now only stands just over 10 ft (3m) high as it has a marked lean to the north. It fell over in 1945, and was re-erected in 1956 after a small excavation had been carried out. This showed that the stone stood in a setting of quartz pebbles below which were two small, shallow hollows; features which have been found to contain human bone or ashes at other, similar, sites.

The open landscape of heath and pasture surrounding the St Breock Downs Monolith contains many other Bronze Age ritual monuments, with which the stone was probably associated. These include at least one other standing stone, and a series of barrows that extend up to 4 miles (7km) to the west.

The fascination of the monolith, also known as the St Breock Longstone or Men Gurta, is reflected by its prominence in local folklore as a medieval and later meeting-place. It occurs in antiquarian records as early as 1613, and was later adopted as a St Breock parish boundary marker.

Ancient and modern monuments on St Breock Downs

On St Breock Downs, 3¾ miles SW of Wadebridge, off unclassified road to Rosenannon *OS Map200; ref SW 968683*

41

St Catherine's Castle seen across the River Fowey estuary from Polruan

St Catherine's Castle is an early artillery fort, probably built during the 1530s. A two-gun battery was added below it in 1855 at the time of the Crimean War, and as late as the Second World War the fort was modified again to form part of a more extensive battery. It demonstrates well how military architecture, technology and defensive tactics developed over a period of 400 years.

The castle formed part of the comprehensive system of coastal defence begun by Henry VIII after his break with the Church of Rome resulted in England's isolation from Catholic Europe. It is shown as part of the defences of Fowey Harbour on a map of 1540 as 'half-made'. The building work was supervised by Thomas Treffry, whose family had played a leading role in the town for several generations. Treffry went on to supervise the building of Pendennis and St Mawes castles in the 1540s, and the design of St Catherine's seems primitive by comparison.

St Catherine's Castle takes its name from the rocky headland on which it stands. Its position, high above the entrance to the Fowey estuary, is spectacular: from the terrace there are superb views across the attractive town and harbour. Fowey, pronounced 'Foye' which was its original name, is built on the steep west bank of the estuary, with a maze of narrow, winding streets. It has a long tradition as a port, and was important enough to be attacked by the French and Spanish in 1380. Before the building of St Catherine's Castle, Fowey harbour had been defended by a chain stretched

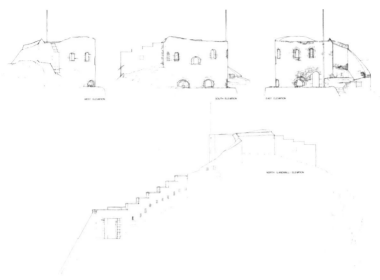

West, south, east and north elevations of the castle

between two square blockhouses. That in Polruan, on the eastern side of the estuary opposite Fowey, still stands to almost its full height, and can be clearly seen from the castle.

The fort consists of a single D-shaped tower looking south-east from the tip of the headland, from which two sections of curtain wall, pierced by musketry slits, extend downslope to the north-east and south-west. A bastion projects outwards from the north-east stretch of wall and there is a wide gateway near its north-east end. Both stretches of wall terminate in precipitous cliffs, cutting off a near semicircular area at the end of the headland.

The tower is two storeys high, with walls up to 4 ft 6 in (1.35m) thick.

The castle on its rocky promontory

boards, rather than on wheels. On the ground floor there are three gunports and a tall, narrow fireplace. At first-floor level there are five narrow windows, which would have been useful as lookout and small arms positions. The one above the entrance is largely blocked, and has a brick oven, now also blocked, built into it. There are two gunports at this level, one now blocked.

In one corner of the tower are the remains of a spiral staircase that gave access to the upper floor and roof, which was probably finished off by a parapet. There are no domestic quarters and it is unlikely that there was ever a permanent garrison stationed here.

St Catherine's Castle was kept in repair throughout the Tudor period and manned during the first English Civil War (1642–6), when Cornwall as a whole declared for

There are two rows of gunports, which cover both the approaches to the estuary and the harbour itself. These gunports have been modified over the years but were originally intended for cannon mounted on flat

the king, but by 1684 it was described as 'ruinous'. In the mid-19th century the fear of invasion returned during the Crimean War, leading to a general refortification of the south coast. At St Catherine's a battery for two guns was built on the levelled platform on the tip of the headland below the fort, protected behind a parapet wall. A magazine was built into the rock beside the curtain wall entrance. The refurbishments were recorded by a series of square granite plaques marked 'WD 1855' and fixed onto the curtain wall and bastion.

By the end of the 19th century St Catherine's Castle had again been abandoned, but it was to be put back into military service once more during the Second World War. From June 1940 St Catherine's Point became a gun battery and observation post, stretching from the castle itself to the higher ground to the west. One of the Crimean War gun emplacements became the site for one of two anti-aircraft guns, and a concrete pillbox was built beside it.

Left: A blocked gunport

Facing page, below: One of the granite plaques commemorating the 19th-century refurbishments

The magazine beside the gateway was brought back into use to store ammunition and the 16th-century tower served as the firing point for a controlled minefield laid across the mouth of the Fowey estuary. Most of the 1940s concrete defences were dismantled after the war, bringing to an end this most recent chapter in the military history of the castle.

¾ mile SW of Fowey along footpath off A3082; 10-min walk, signposted from Readymoney Cove car park (Fowey)
OS Map 200;
ref SX 119509

45

Cornwall's earliest known burial monuments are its chambered tombs, known locally as quoits. Also found in Wales, Scotland, Ireland and Brittany, where they are generally dated to the earlier Neolithic (*c* 4000–3500 BC), Cornish examples continued to be a focus for ritual and burial well into the Bronze Age (*c* 2500–750 BC). Though crude in design – stone-slab boxes topped by massive capstones – their construction

Above: *Ballowall Barrow*

Facing page: *The huge capstone of Trethevy Quoit*

would have required great ingenuity and communal effort. Antiquarian accounts of these monuments mention floors strewn with bones, suggesting perhaps that the tombs were used for communal burial. Access to them, however, was intended to be difficult. The spaces between the slabs were often blocked and several, such as Chun, Zennor and Lanyon Quoits, were surrounded by earthen mounds. Most rituals may therefore have taken place in front of the chambers with entry restricted to a chosen few people and occasions.

Some time in the later Neolithic or Early Bronze Age entrance graves came into use. These are a type of passage grave – circular mounds containing a passage leading to one or more chambers – found only in the far west of Cornwall and Scilly. At their most basic, entrance graves consisted of low rectangular or coffin-shaped stone chambers, roofed with small stone slabs. Originally open at one end, they were easily accessible, indicating that they were intended to be actively used; probably for ceremonies associated with the deposition of the dead. They range in design from small, apparently single-phase, sites such as Brane, Sancreed, to massive structures like Ballowall Barrow. Many were extensively remodelled which suggests that they were in use for a long period. At the end of their ritual lives the chambers were deliberately sealed.

Perhaps the most numerous reminders of Cornwall's prehistoric past are the barrows and cairns (earth or stone mounds) that dot its hills, cliffs and heaths. Ranging in date from the later Neolithic to the Middle Bronze Age (c 3000–1000 BC), they gradually replaced the earlier types of burial monument. Many had long and complex histories, sometimes remaining in use for several centuries. Most barrows began as a circular enclosure marked by a ditch, an earth bank or an arrangement of posts or stones. These enclosures were then the focus of ritual activities including the deposition of pottery, metalwork and animal or human remains. The latter could take the form of complete bodies, stretched out or curled in the foetal position, and accompanied by personal possessions such as beads, stone tools or, occasionally, bronze daggers. In most cases, however, the interments consisted of cremated bone,

usually contained within or beneath an urn. Many sites were then covered by earthen or stone mounds, sometimes with further cremations placed within the mounds themselves.

Not all barrows contained human remains, however, and it would be wrong to see them as being exclusively burial monuments. Nor were they the only means of disposing of the dead – human remains have also been found adjacent to standing stones, beneath settlement remains, and even wedged within natural rock crevices. Barrows also clearly acted as visible markers within the landscape and may in some cases have demarcated territory. Whatever their intended function they remain as significant today, as distinctive and evocative elements of the Cornish landscape, as they were to the communities that built them.

Tregiffian is a type of chambered tomb known as an entrance grave, and survives largely intact, despite the levelling of part of its mound to make a road in the 1840s.

Entrance graves are funerary and ritual monuments dating to the later Neolithic, Early and Middle Bronze Age (c 3000–1000 BC). Of 93 recorded examples in England, 79 are on the Isles of Scilly, and the remainder are confined to the Penwith peninsula at the western tip of Cornwall; they are also found on the Channel Islands and in Brittany.

Right: Entrance and kerb at Tregiffian

Facing page, left: The cast of the cup-marked slab at the entrance

Such tombs typically comprise a roughly circular mound of heaped rubble and earth built over a rectangular chamber, which is constructed from slabs set edge to edge, or rubble walling, and roofed with further slabs. The few entrance graves that have been systematically excavated have revealed cremated human bone and funerary urns, usually within the chambers but occasionally within the mound. However, it is by no means certain that they were solely – or even primarily – burial places. Some may have been shrines at which various religious rituals and ceremonies were performed.

Tregiffian is a large entrance grave, with a low, narrow stone-lined chamber; what survives is about two-thirds of the original structure of the chamber. Internally the chamber measures 16 ft (4.9m) long by up to 6 ft (1.9m) wide and 3 ft (0.9m) high. The walls are built from a combination of edge-set slabs and roughly coursed slabs and rubble.

Four massive slabs or capstones span the chamber width to form the roof. The entrance, at the south-west end, is constricted to 2 ft 7 in (0.8m) wide by two 'portal' slabs: one of these is most unusual, as its face is entirely covered by a network of 25 carved hollows – a rare form of prehistoric rock carving called cup marks. This example may be the oldest in the south west. The slab here is a cast of the original, which has been moved for safe keeping to the Royal Cornwall Museum at Truro.

Another unusual feature of the tomb's construction is the kerb, which was renewed at least once during the

time when the grave was in use. Kerbs of stone slabs are usually found at entrance graves and were designed to retain the earth of the covering mound. Here at Tregiffian the kerb has more prominent slabs facing the chamber entrance, which seems to suggest a deliberate and symbolic blocking.

When the grave was excavated in the 1870s, ashes and bone fragments were found. Further excavations in the 1960s and 1970s uncovered more bone fragments and two pits, one of which contained an intact funerary collared urn.

Tregiffian did not stand alone in its landscape. Close by is a circle of standing stones called the Merry Maidens, of roughly similar date, while other nearby mounds, standing stones and funerary cists are a reminder that this area was a focus for ceremonies and rituals for a thousand years or more.

The massive capstone over the chamber entrance

2 miles SE of St Buryan on B3315; park by the sign to the Merry Maidens, ¼ mile E
OS Map 203; ref SW 431244

Trethevy Quoit is a particularly well-preserved example of a portal dolmen, a type of monument once common in Cornwall and dating to the early or middle part of the Neolithic period, *c* 3500–2500 BC. These distinctive structures are found mainly in the far west of Cornwall but this one, on the southern edge of Bodmin Moor, is perhaps the finest.

Below: The massive capstone from inside the quoit

Facing page, right: Trethevy Quoit

It consists of five standing stones, surmounted by a massive capstone. The capstone may have been designed to be slightly tilted, but now slopes at a much steeper angle than it would have done originally, because the most westerly of the supporting stones has collapsed and lies within the tomb chamber itself. There is a hole near the highest corner of the capstone that appears to be man-made. The whole structure stands 9 ft (2.7m) high and was probably originally covered by a mound or cairn: the chamber is surrounded by the clear remains of a low mound on all sides, apart from at the entrance. This was at the east end, where the stones form a sort of antechamber, but it is not clear how the chamber was reached from outside the original mound.

The contents of this box-like chamber were removed long ago. At the few portal dolmens that have been excavated, pits and post holes have been recorded within and in front of the chamber, containing charcoal and

cremated bone. Many portal dolmens were reused for urned cremations, especially during the Middle Bronze Age.

It is far from certain that these structures were tombs rather than multipurpose shrines. The presence of the dead is no guarantee of the original usage, as is shown by medieval churches: these contain tombs and are surrounded by graves, yet they were built primarily as places where the living could worship. It may be that in prehistoric times the ancestral dead were considered to be mediators between the community and its gods, and that places like this were an important interface between these two worlds.

These burial monuments of Britain's early farming communities are among the oldest visible monuments to survive to the present

day. It is probable that each community once possessed at least one such 'house of the dead', and the time and energy they must have taken to build is an indication of the importance that must have been attached to them. The huge capstone here weighs about 20 tonnes, and manoeuvring it into position was a considerable feat of engineering.

1 mile NE of St Cleer near Darite, off B3254 OS Map 201; ref SX 259688

ISLES OF SCILLY

Once part of a much larger landmass that has submerged gradually with rising sea levels since the Bronze Age, the Isles of Scilly took their current form in historical times. The lack of winter frosts here helps exotic plants and wildlife to thrive and the islands are home to a remarkable number of archaeological and historic sites. Ritual burial monuments, cist grave cemeteries and Romano-Celtic settlements – such as those seen at Halangy Down on St Mary's – provide evidence that a distinctive Scillonian culture has occupied the island group for over 4,000 years. An important and unusual range of post-medieval

Cromwell's Castle and the strait between Tresco and Bryher

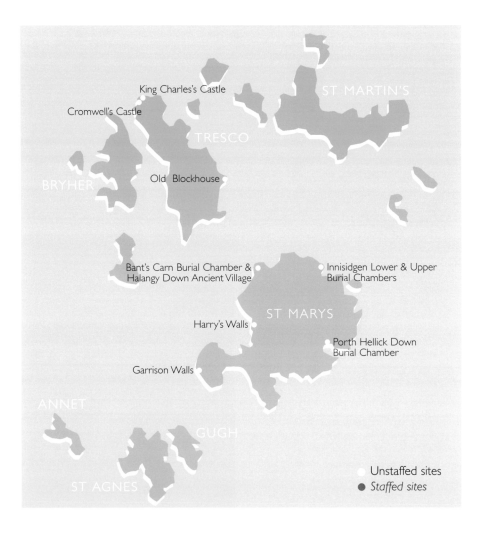

King Charles's Castle

Cromwell's Castle

ST MARTIN'S

TRESCO

BRYHER

Old Blockhouse

Bant's Carn Burial Chamber & Halangy Down Ancient Village

Innisidgen Lower & Upper Burial Chambers

ST MARYS

Harry's Walls

Porth Hellick Down Burial Chamber

Garrison Walls

ANNET

GUGH

○ Unstaffed sites
● *Staffed sites*

ST AGNES

53

PORT, TOWN PIER & HARBOUR of ST MARYS in SCILLY with the NORTHERN ISLANDS taken from BOSOU HILL June 2.1752.

Honorabilis Franciscus Godolphin de Baylies in Com: Buck: Armiger hanc tabulam impensis suis ære incisam suo nomine decorari voluit.

monuments stand as testament to the strategic importance of the Isles of Scilly; not least the Garrison Walls on St Mary's, begun in Elizabeth I's reign and continually updated and adapted for successive conflicts right up to the Second World War. The islands' rocky shores have long been acknowledged as a shipping hazard and have played an important role in the development of navigational aids.

Above: St Mary's with the northern isles in the background (1752)

Right: Innisidgen Lower burial chamber, St Mary's

Facing page: Porth Hellick Down burial chamber, St Mary's

The coastal slopes of Halangy Down are home to a wide range of well-preserved and interrelated remains from prehistoric to Roman times. Bant's Carn, a Bronze Age tomb of the type known as an entrance grave, sits on the crest of the hill. On the slopes below lie the remains of an Iron Age settlement that continued in use for about 500 years until the end of the Roman period. Between and around the two monuments are the extensive remains of prehistoric field systems.

There is evidence of extensive and permanent settlement on the Isles of Scilly from around 2500 BC. At that time the sea level was lower and much of Scilly formed a single landmass. Throughout later prehistory the sea level continued to rise, and it was probably at about the end of the Roman period that the islands we see today began to form, when the sea had flooded the productive farmlands that presumably occupied the sheltered valleys and flatter lands between the present islands.

Bant's Carn

About 80 stone structures known as entrance graves are recorded from this period on the Isles of Scilly. Such a concentration in a small area is very unusual, and Bant's Carn is one of

The entrance to Bant's Carn

the finest of these monuments.
It consists of an outer platform
surrounding an inner cairn or mound
containing a slab-built chamber. The
mound is about 26 ft (8m) long and
20 ft (6m) wide, retained by a
well-made kerb of stone slabs; a
second kerb retains the lower
platform around the mound. The
mound may once have been more
than 13 ft (4m) high, so that it would
have entirely covered the boat-shaped,
stone-lined burial chamber whose
roof is now exposed. The chamber
itself, 17 ft (5.25 m) long by 5 ft
(1.5 m) wide, is much higher than
most other entrance graves – up to
5 ft (1.5 m) in places – and is roofed
with four enormous capstones. A
stone-lined entrance passage, now
roofless, leads from the outer kerb to
the entrance of the burial chamber.

Bant's Carn was excavated in
1900, but was found to be almost
empty. At the far end of the burial
chamber four piles of cremated
human bones were discovered,
together with a few fragments of

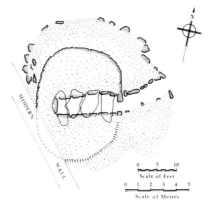

*Plan of the
burial chamber*

decorated pottery. Most of these were
probably from the urns in which the
remains of the dead had originally
been placed, but one was part of a
shallow bowl, much older than
the rest and perhaps dating back to
the time of the very first settlers.
More pottery of a similar kind was
discovered in 1970 during the
re-erection of a fallen capstone.

The high number and concentration
of entrance graves found on the Isles
of Scilly have led some archaeologists
to suggest that the practice of
communal burial may have continued

The ancient village on Halangy Down

graves in the care of English Heritage can be seen at Innisidgen and Porth Hellick Down on St Mary's.

Halangy Down Ancient Village

The later-Iron Age to Roman settlement lies below Bant's Carn at the south-west edge of Halangy Down. Between the two and on the slope to the north-east, traces of prehistoric field systems are visible as a series of terraces and banks, generally following the contours of the slopes. Some of the stone slabs used to retain the terraces can still be seen, and individual terraces survive to a length of about 330 yds (300m). The banks intersecting the terraces and running down some parts of the Halangy Downslope are later modifications that created smaller rectangular field plots.

much longer here than on the mainland. It may be that fewer examples have survived on the mainland because land was in short supply. It has also been suggested that these monuments may have acted as territorial markers, signifying ancestral ownership: many of them, like Bant's Carn, stand close to prehistoric field systems that were already in existence when the mounds were built. Other Scillonian entrance

The Iron Age and Romano-British inhabitants of the settlement here probably lived in much the same way as their Bronze Age predecessors. Excavation in the 1950s revealed a complex of 11 inter-connecting stone-built houses, most of them simple oval structures. Post holes show that each house had its own conical thatched roof; there were stone-lined drains, and stores or cupboards constructed within the thickness of the walls. One house, larger than the rest, was built on the courtyard pattern characteristic of the surviving Romano-British villages on the mainland in west Cornwall, good examples of which are Carn Euny and Chysauster. These houses are arranged with various rooms leading off a small courtyard, all contained within a massive enclosing wall and entered via a narrow passage. The house at Halangy Down is 90 ft (27m) long by up to 48 ft (14.5 m) wide, with three rooms and a long, curved entrance passage.

All the houses showed signs of repair and alteration, suggesting that the settlement had a long and vigorous life. Excavations at the site produced many artefacts and showed that the inhabitants practised a mixed economy, farming cattle, sheep, pigs and horses. Apart from a few scraps of Samian ware – glazed red pottery imported from southern Gaul – there was little sign of contact with the outside world. Despite living through the rise and fall of the Roman Empire, the people of Halangy Down had little reason to be concerned with events across the sea.

The inhabitants of this later settlement appear to have been buried individually, rather than in large collective tombs like Bant's Carn: west of the Halangy Down settlement is a cemetery of small funerary chambers called cists, of a form typical of the Romano-British period in Scilly.

The remains of an Iron Age house, Halangy Down

On St Mary's, 1 mile N of Hugh Town; from coastguard station follow signposted track towards coast and fork right *OS map 203; ref SV 910123 (entrance grave); SV 910124 (settlement)*

59

'The Last Giantess': giants Cormoran and Trecrobben sharing a hammer, which fell and killed Cormoran's wife.

These western lands have many secret and sacred places. As changeable as the weather, at once both enchanting and treacherous, they are lands of contrast and mystery. Their isolation meant that old ways and old tales clung on long after they had been forgotten elsewhere; Thomas Hardy's description of a place 'pre-eminently the region of dream and mystery' still holds true. Despite Cornwall being at the forefront of the Industrial Revolution it remained a place of scattered rural hamlets and in the mining districts superstition was rife and folktales well known. Folklorists such as William Bottrell, Robert Hunt and Margaret Courtney published rich collections of folktales and legends at the end of the 19th century, which are still in print.

These stories are the 'song-lines' of Cornwall and Scilly. They tell how the land was shaped by giants, King Arthur and the Devil. There are tales about the fairy-folk, the mermaids, witches, piskies (Cornish pixies), and knockers (the goblins of the mines). Iron Age tunnels or fogous appear frequently in Cornish folklore; some were reputed to be the haunt of malevolent spirits guarding treasure. Bottrell was told that smugglers had invented these fearful stories to keep prying people from discovering their contraband.

The wild setting of Tintagel Castle has long been an inspiration for the legend of King Arthur. Geoffrey of Monmouth in the 1130s was the first to associate Arthur with the castle, telling how Uther Pendragon assumed the form of the Duke Gorlois, whose beautiful wife Igraine he then seduced. The wizard Merlin raised the boy in secret. Other local sites are associated with the legend; Dozmary Pool on Bodmin Moor, some say, is where Sir Bedivere threw the dying king's sword, Excalibur. The Arthurian stories have inspired writers, artists and poets through the centuries and continue to do so; the bards in the annual Cornish Gorseth still say '*Nyns yu marow Myghtem Arthur!*': 'King Arthur is not dead!'

The Isles of Scilly are known as the Fortunate Isles, the last vestiges of the lost land of Lyonesse. They were home to one of Arthur's knights, Tristan or Tristram, son of King Meliodas of Lyonesse and nephew of King Mark of Cornwall. Mark

sent Tristan to Ireland to fetch the Irish king's daughter, Yseult, to be his wife, but instead Tristan fell in love with her after the pair drank a love potion. Their love endured many adventures and, as might be expected, the tale ends tragically. One version has it that Tristan was stabbed by Mark in the back; another that he died of grief when falsely told that Yseult had abandoned him. An inscription on the Drustanus Stone near Fowey in Cornwall, sometimes called the 'Tristan Stone', is thought by some to commemorate this tale. Tintagel features again, as home to King Mark's court,

Above: *Ann Jefferies and the fairies, from J E Smith's* Legends and Miracles, *1837*

Left: *Sir Tristram at King Arthur's court, from* The Pageant of British History, *1909*

John Norden's 1650 engraving of Roche Rock, where Jan Tregeagle sought sanctuary from demon hounds

when Tristan and Yseult's story first appears in writing.

Ballowall Barrow, also known as Carn Gluze, has long been said to be a fairy place; tin miners in the past saw strange lights there as they went home in the evening. The small people, or 'pobel vean', were also seen by housemaid Ann Jefferies in the late 17th century and her employer Moses Pitt wrote to the Bishop of Gloucester about her case in 1696. These 'small sort of airy people' fed her from harvest to the next Christmas Day and she wasn't seen to eat any normal food. When she was imprisoned without food in Bodmin Gaol the fairies fed her,

and continued to help her after her release, when she administered herbal remedies.

John (Jan) Tregeagle was a venal and corrupt landlord and magistrate to whom ancient tales of a tormented spirit have become attached. After an evil life Tregeagle was condemned to carry out impossible tasks to earn redemption for his dreadful deeds in life. His first was to drain the bottomless Dozmary Pool with a holed limpet shell, but when a terrible storm drove him from the pool he fled, pursued by demon hounds. He sought sanctuary at Roche Rock chapel but could only get his head in through the window, leaving the rest of him to their savage teeth. Saved by the local priest, he was then condemned to weave rope from sand and finally taken in chains to carry the sand from Berepper beach to Porthleven. Tripped up one night by demons, a sack of sand fell from his back and formed Loe Bar. Tregeagle toils to this day at Land's End, sweeping the sands from Porthcurno Cove to Mill Bay; his howls are terrible when the gales drive it back again.

Facing page: Tintagel, on its rocky promontory, has inspired Arthurian legends for centuries

CROMWELL'S CASTLE

History

This tall round tower sits on a low projecting shelf of rock and commands the channel between Tresco and Bryher. It is one of only a few stone fortifications that survive from the Interregnum (1649–60) and takes its name from Oliver Cromwell, Lord Protector of England during this period between the reigns of Charles I and Charles II. The fort replaced a Tudor blockhouse on the site, and superseded King Charles's Castle, which had been built in the 1550s on higher ground but proved

to be poorly sited and was partly demolished to provide building stone for this later castle.

Royalists had held out on the Isles of Scilly for most of the Civil War period. Increasing tension with the Dutch, and in particular the arrival of a Dutch fleet off the islands in March 1651 demanding reparations from the Royalist privateers based there, prompted Parliament to send Robert Blake, the most successful admiral of the 17th century, to recapture these strategic islands.

The castle was built in 1651, following swiftly on Blake's success, to guard one of the main routes of entry to the heart of the islands and the deep water approach to New Grimsby harbour. It faced a potential enemy with an impossible choice. No fleet could hope to land troops on this side of Tresco unless it had first destroyed or captured the castle, but the chances of destroying the castle by gunfire from the sea were very slim. The fort was considered worth updating a century later, when a

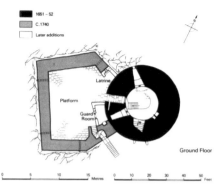

platform for cannon was added on the seaward side.

Description

The castle consisted of a basement, two upper storeys and a gun platform on the roof. The rubble walls below the platform are almost 13 ft (4m) thick; internally the tower measures nearly 20 ft (6m) across and is over 50 ft (15m) high. The original entrance, later blocked, was high up on the south side, reached by external wooden stairs: stone supports or corbels, projecting out from the doorway, would have supported a wooden platform in front of it. The roof survives, supported by a fine ribbed vault, and although the intervening floors have gone their positions are evident from joist holes and fireplaces. The basement was presumably intended for storage. A spiral staircase within the walls takes the visitor up to the roof, where the six widely splayed gunports give an all-round field of fire.

On the south-west side of the tower, facing the sea, is the large 18th-century gun platform that replaced the original gun battery. The gun platform, designed for six cannon, is surrounded by a low parapet wall. To provide better access to the tower the original entrance was made into a window and a new one made from the platform. The rooms on either side of the later entrance – a guardroom with a fireplace to the right, and a latrine to the left – are also 18th-century additions.

On Tresco, 1 mile NW of New Grimsby by footpath. Approach with care. *OS Map 203; ref SV 882159*

65

*The defences around
The Garrison,
St Mary's*

History

The defences of The Garrison on St Mary's form one of the most remarkable and impressive coastal defence systems in England. They span 350 years: the first stretch of curtain wall, built after the defeat of the Spanish Armada in 1588, was

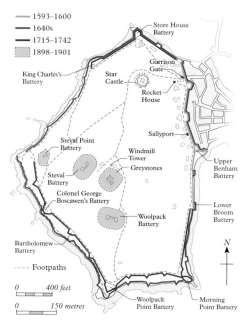

- ▬ 1593–1600
- ▬ 1640s
- ▬ 1715–1742
- ▨ 1898–1901

Store House Battery
Garrison Gate
King Charles's Battery
Star Castle
Rocket House
Steval Point Battery
Sallyport
Windmill Tower
Greystones
Steval Battery
Upper Benham Battery
Colonel George Boscawen's Battery
Lower Broom Battery
Woolpack Battery
Bartholomew Battery
- ---- Footpaths
N
0   400 feet
0   150 metres
Woolpack Point Battery
Morning Point Battery

rebuilt and extended around the headland in the 18th century, and the fortifications here were still being put to military use during the Second World War.

Scilly was recognised as a possible base for attacks on shipping from the 1550s onwards, but during much of the reign of Queen Elizabeth I (1558–1603) the islands' defences were neglected. Nothing was done to strengthen them before the attack of the Armada in 1588, but the probability that King Philip of Spain would send a second armada made it vital to take action. For some years the islands had been leased to the Cornish Godolphin family, and it was the head of this family and governor of the islands, Sir Francis Godolphin, who was given the task of constructing new fortifications.

The site chosen was The Hugh, a prominent headland jutting out to the west from St Mary's. The nucleus of the scheme was Star Castle, built in 1593–4 (now a hotel). To protect it on the landward side, a length of curtain wall was built across the neck of the headland from coast to coast, with four bastions and a fortified entrance. Godolphin took his responsibilities seriously, and in 1595 expressed his concerns that 'the gathering of these Spaniards seemeth as a cloud that is like to fall'.

The Spanish threat never materialised but during the English Civil War the Royalists initially held the Isles of Scilly and in March 1646 the future Charles II stayed on the island for a few weeks before slipping away to the safety of Jersey. The Royalists surrendered to Parliament the following September, but after a revolt two years later The Garrison again became a Royalist stronghold, and a base for up to 800 men. Finally, in 1651, the Parliamentarian Admiral Blake, after capturing Tresco, turned the full force of his guns on The Hugh, forcing a Royalist surrender.

Invasion by France or Spain remained a possibility during the 17th and early 18th centuries. The Elizabethan curtain wall was gradually extended until it surrounded almost the whole of the headland, with bastions covering every possible angle of approach from sea or land. The Godolphins remained in charge, with most of the major work being carried out between 1715 and 1742 under the supervision of Abraham Tovey, the resident master gunner. Many of the surviving buildings on The Hugh date from this time, including workshops, stores and houses as well as defensive structures. It was during this period that the concentration of defences on The Hugh led to it becoming known as The Garrison.

Further strengthening of the headland took place between 1898 and 1901, when the massive Woolpack and Steval batteries were added, with the Greystones Barracks between them. Between 1902 and 1906 these were

Garrison Gateway by Jessie Mothersole, from The Isles of Scilly, *1910*

GARRISON WALLS

Looking north-west along the walls towards Colonel Boscawen's Battery

supplemented by the Steval Point Battery and, on the north-west coast of St Mary's, the Bant's Carn Battery, built for quick-firing guns. The Garrison was used again in the First World War, when it was re-armed and accommodated almost 1,000 servicemen. In the Second World War the Isles of Scilly were at the forefront of the Battle of the Atlantic. Large numbers of servicemen were again stationed here and The Garrison was an important signal station, with pillboxes cleverly constructed within the 18th-century batteries.

The Garrison Walls and Rocket House magazine are in the care of English Heritage.

Description

The fortifications of The Garrison are very well preserved, and visitors today can walk much of the length of the Garrison Walls (the north-eastern stretch between Garrison Gate and Store House Battery is not open to the public).

The Tudor curtain wall across the neck of The Hugh, dating to about 1600, is built from large granite blocks; a deep rock-cut ditch is visible in places along the town side, although this is partly silted up. This part of the wall and its batteries were partly rebuilt in the 18th century, when Abraham Tovey extended the defensive scheme around most of the headland. Note the contrast between the well-cut ashlar blocks of the 18th-century walls and the rougher masonry of the Tudor section. At Garrison Gate, the original arched gateway survives, as remodelled by Tovey with a bellcote and parapet above, together with barracks on either side and a guardhouse. The initials GR, FG and AT, and the date 1742, commemorate the work – the initials are those of King George, Francis Godolphin and Tovey himself.

Just beyond the gate is a sunken powder magazine, later called the Rocket House. Tovey surrounded this 17th-century structure with a massive blast-protection wall; a wise precaution at a time when accidents with explosives were not uncommon. A small prison cell adjoins the outer side of the blast-wall's entrance. The magazine now houses an exhibition about The Garrison's history.

Beyond the magazine and Star Castle, the defences of The Garrison, together with barracks, stores and workshops, are spread out across the headland. The 18th-century walls extend all around the headland apart from its north-west coast; the stone-faced earthen bank and inner ditch, or breastwork, running along the clifftop is a remarkable survival from the Civil War.

Large 18th-century bastions along the curtain wall were designed to cover the main sea approaches, while the higher slopes of the headland are dominated by the early-20th-century batteries that were built to counter attacks from enemy cruisers and torpedo boats. Of the latter, only Woolpack Battery is now accessible. The tower near the centre of the headland was a 16th-century windmill, rebuilt as a gun tower and converted into a signal station in the 1870s: it is now in private use. The cannon on display at several of the batteries date from the 18th and early 19th centuries.

The entrance to Woolpack Battery

On St Mary's. From Hugh Town follow the road west around the headland to the Garrison Gate
OS Map 203; ref SV 898104

Two of Cornwall's great native writers were born in St Austell. Historian and poet A L Rowse featured local themes in several of his works, including the autobiographical *A Cornish Childhood*. Poet and novelist Jack Clemo, the son of a china-clay quarry worker, recreated the grim landscape of the clay pits in his collections *The Map of Clay* and *The Echoing Tip*.

Daphne du Maurier made her home on the Fowey peninsula and her house, Menabilly, was the Manderley of her most famous novel, *Rebecca*, first published in 1938. The twelve novels of Winston Graham's *Poldark* series are set in real and fictional 18th-century Cornish towns

around Perranporth and St Agnes.

'Cornish Wonder' John Opie was born in St Agnes in 1761. Opie was an outstanding portraitist, particularly of children and elderly women. J M W Turner visited Cornwall in 1811 and Tintagel was among his many subjects, as was St Ives – the town that was to become a mecca for artists. J M Whistler and W R Sickert established studios there in 1884, using converted sail lofts at Porthmeor Beach. Meanwhile, Alexander Stanhope Forbes and Walter Langley had become the focus of a school of artists at Newlyn, and a second generation of artists continued to work there well into the 20th century.

In the 1920s Bernard Leach established his famous pottery at St Ives, producing stoneware from local materials. Soon after, artists Ben Nicholson and Christopher

Above: Jack Clemo, photographed in 1975 by Derek Parker
Left: A Gentleman and a Miner with a Specimen of Copper Ore, by John Opie (1761–1807)

Wood settled in St Ives. A colony of avant-garde landscape-inspired artists and sculptors grew up there, including local 'primitive' artist Alfred Wallis. In the 1940s Barbara Hepworth set up her studio there, and the post-war generation of St Ives artists included Peter Lanyon and Bryan Wynter. Tate St Ives continues to stimulate the arts of the region.

The countless shipwrecks off the coast of the Isles of Scilly were a particular inspiration to Scillonian poet Robert Maybee. A working-class poet, Maybee's *Sixty-eight Years Experience in the Scilly Isles* appeared in 1884. Scilly-born novelist Sam Llewellyn uses local settings, too, for thrillers such as *Hell Bay* and *The Sea Garden*.

The varied events in the lives of the islanders have been captured on camera by five generations of Scillonian photographers. John Gibson first began recording local life in the 1860s, and his great-grandson Frank published a later vision of the islands in his 1980 book *My Scillonian Home. A Century of Images*, a collection of the Gibsons' photographs, was published in 1997 and the family continues to record every aspect of life on the Isles of Scilly and West Cornwall.

Above: *Flower farmers on St Mary's, photographed by Alexander Gibson*
Left: *Landscape with Field and Cottages, c1928, by Alfred Wallis*

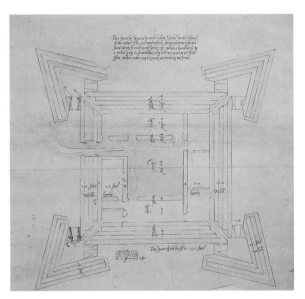

16th-century plan for Harry's Walls, now at Hatfield House

History

These two artillery bastions and length of curtain wall belong to an unfinished fort, begun – despite its name – in 1551, during the reign of King Edward VI (1547–53).

Under Henry VIII (reigned 1509–47), a new generation of powerful guns was beginning to change the nature of warfare.

Unfortunately for England, this was just at the time when the king's break with Rome made the south coast vulnerable to attack from France or Spain. Henry's response was to order the building of a chain of artillery forts and blockhouses to guard the harbours and beaches of southern England. However, despite the strategic importance of the Isles of Scilly at the entrance to the English Channel, no major works were undertaken there before Henry died, though he had sent 150 soldiers to guard them. They were garrisoned at Ennor Castle, which commanded the harbour at Old Town on St Mary's.

In 1551 Edward VI's government found the money to begin building a much more up-to-date fort, the remains of which are now known as Harry's Walls. This seems to have been an early attempt to mount heavy guns to protect the approaches to Hugh Town, where rising sea levels had opened up a large, sheltered harbour.

To be effective, a fort had to command the widest possible field of fire for its own guns, while affording adequate protection against the guns of the enemy. Although Harry's Walls was built on high ground, it quickly became apparent to the builders that this was not the best place from which to prevent an attack on the harbour. The headland now known as The Garrison offered a better location, and was eventually chosen as the site of the islands' principal fortress, Star Castle, in the 1590s. In the interim, however, attention shifted to Tresco and the building of King Charles's Castle as the main stronghold for the islands.

Description

A surviving plan of the fort shows that it was originally designed to be square, with large, pointed bastions at each corner, and with internal buildings ranging along all four sides of the curtain wall; a mill and brewhouse were to be built by the freshwater pond below the hill. In the event only the two south-westerly bastions were completed, together

with the connecting stretch of curtain wall, 89 ft (27m) long. The structure has been heavily robbed of its dressed stone. The acutely angled, or arrow-headed, bastions were designed to offer maximum coverage of the walls between them, and to present the narrowest possible front to enemy fire. Had it been completed, Harry's Walls would have been one of the first artillery forts in England to feature these bastions – first developed in Italy during the late 15th century – preceding the much better known works at Carisbrooke Castle on the Isle of Wight and at Berwick-on-Tweed by some years.

A trench marks the planned line of the north-west curtain wall, and just beyond it is a tall standing stone sitting within a low cairn, probably of Bronze Age date (*c* 2500–750 BC).

The unfinished walls of the fort

On St Mary's, above Porth Mellon beach, ½ mile NE of Hugh Town by footpath
OS Map 203; ref SV 909109

73

The substantial kerb and massive capstones of the Upper Burial Chamber

The Isles of Scilly are rich in monuments of the Bronze Age (*c* 2500–750 BC), a time when permanent settlers, probably from west Cornwall, began farming here on a large scale. They built ceremonial monuments on hilltops and coastal plateaux, and among the most impressive of these are the chambered tombs or entrance graves, of which the two at Innisidgen are fine examples.

Entrance graves are often described as Scillonian tombs because of their concentration on the islands: although a few are found on the Penwith peninsula of west Cornwall. They are quite uniform in plan. Most comprise a roughly circular mound

retained by a stone kerb, and built over a rectangular, stone-lined chamber which is roofed with large granite slabs. Some of the mounds are set within a large, kerbed platform.

Those entrance graves that have been excavated have contained cremated human bone and funerary urns – one such tomb, Knackyboy Carn on St Martin's, was found to contain the cremated remains of at least 60 individuals. Entrance graves seem to have continued in use on Scilly long after individual burial had become the usual practice on the mainland. It is possible that the monuments may also have served much wider ritual and social functions, perhaps as territorial markers for the land of the founding kin groups and as places where offerings might be made.

The two entrance graves at Innisidgen were constructed on a hill overlooking a wide valley. Beside and below, filling the valley bottom, were walled fields. Their present position beside the coast is the result of the rise in sea level that took place over many hundreds of years. Both sites were empty when first entered in modern times.

The upper Innisidgen burial chamber, or Innisidgen Carn, is one of the best preserved entrance graves on Scilly. The mound measures 30 ft (9m) by 26 ft (8m), and is currently about 6 ft (2m) high. The surrounding wall or kerb is substantial: nearly 3 ft (1m) high on the north side. Slight traces of an outer platform, up to 6 ft (2m) wide, surround the mound. A short, open passage on the eastern side leads to the entrance, which is covered by a massive slab. Four further

capstones make up the roof of a rectangular burial chamber 15 ft (4.5m) long and about 5 ft (1.5m) high.

Lower Innisidgen entrance grave, 300 ft (90m) to the north-west, is more damaged and retains only two of its capstones. Parts of the kerb of the mound survive, while the mound itself incorporates outcrops of rock. The entrance to the chamber is on the south side.

A prehistoric field system survives on the northern slope of the hill adjoining the entrance graves, visible as earth and rubble banks. The association of such funerary monuments with the farming landscape is a distinctive feature of the Isles of Scilly.

Left: Two massive capstones survive at the Lower Burial Chamber

Below: The Lower Burial Chamber and mound

On St Mary's, 1¾ miles NE of Hugh Town; well signposted along coastal path, half way between Watermill Cove and Bar Point
OS Map 203; ref SV 922127

History

Although taking its name from its occupation by Royalist forces in 1651, this small artillery fort was probably built 100 years earlier, during the reign of King Edward VI (1547–53). It was intended to protect the narrow strait leading past New Grimsby harbour and on towards St Mary's, but proved to be badly sited to withstand attack or to fire on ships in the channel below – its guns would have to point down at so steep an angle to hit ships in New Grimsby

View from the hall

Channel that the cannonballs would have rolled out of the cannons before they fired.

After an abortive attempt in 1551 to build an artillery fort on St Mary's, the remains of which are now known as Harry's Walls, Edward VI's engineers focused instead on strengthening Tresco. Paradoxically, the design of King Charles's Castle seems to look backward, recalling the angular gun forts built during King Henry's reign, whereas the arrow-headed bastions of the unfinished Harry's Walls resembled those found in the most up-to-date forts in Italy and the Low Countries.

Despite its initial importance, King Charles's Castle was soon superseded as the islands' chief stronghold by Star Castle on The Garrison, St Mary's, in the 1590s. The main reason seems to have been the castle's poor position, perched on a crest 40m above sea level. It was garrisoned by the Royalists during the Civil War, but when the Parliamentarians took Tresco in 1651 they simply bypassed

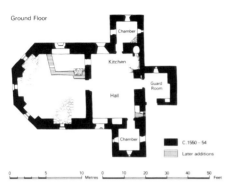

Ground Floor

Chamber

Kitchen

Guard Room

Hall

Chamber

■ C.1550 – 54
▤ Later additions

0 5 10 Metres
0 10 20 30 40 50 Feet

the castle by landing on the other side of the island. The castle seems to have been partially dismantled to provide stone for Cromwell's Castle which was built on lower ground.

Description

Despite its partial demolition, the plan of the castle is reasonably clear. Cruciform in shape, it was originally two storeys high. It is entered on the eastern side by a guardroom. An arched doorway, which still has its drawbar slot, leads into a big rectangular hall which has two large fireplaces: one contains a bread oven,

suggesting that this part of the main living space was partitioned off as a kitchen. Two small chambers at either end were probably sleeping quarters.

A doorway in the centre of the west wall of the hall leads onto the ground floor of the semi-hexagonal gun platform. Five gunports survive at ground level, and two on the upper storey have been reconstructed.

During the Civil War period (1642–51) attempts were made to strengthen the fort on its vulnerable landward side by means of a new earth-and-stone rampart. The much-eroded remains of further outworks can be traced eastwards across Castle Down, where a large bastion of uncertain date is set amid prehistoric cairns and field systems.

Above: King Charles's Castle
Left: Ground-floor plan of the castle

On Tresco, ¾ mile NW of New Grimsby by footpath. Approach with care. OS Map 203; ref SV 882161

77

Tales of dramatic shipwrecks are a distinctive feature of the history of the Isles of Scilly, and with good reason. The islands' reefs and rocky coastlines reach into the Western Approaches, threatening long-established maritime routes linking north-west Europe with the rest of the world. This danger was recognised even by Romans – a shrine on the island of Nornour is believed to have been erected by Roman sailors grateful for a safe landfall.

Rudimentary navigational methods and inaccurate charts increased the dangers to early seafarers. A British fleet under Admiral Sir Clowdisley Shovell, returning from besieging Toulon on 22 October 1707, was driven onto Scilly's Western Rocks as a result of a navigational error.

Four ships sank, including the flagship *Association*, with the loss of over 1,640 lives: it was England's worst maritime disaster. A memorial marks the place where Shovell's body washed ashore at Porth Hellick on St Mary's.

In the following century even the manoeuvrability of steamships did not guarantee safe passage. In May 1875 the liner *Schiller* struck the Retarrier Ledges in the Western Rocks in fog, with the loss of 311 of her 355 passengers and crew. The churchyard in Old Town, St Mary's, has several poignant memorials of those who were buried there.

Though the loss of life was tragic, recovered cargoes undoubtedly provided unpredictable boosts to the economy of the

islands. Samples from the cargo cast overboard to refloat SS *Minnehaha*, grounded on Scilly Rock in 1910, still reputedly adorns some households. Many would have been delighted to acquire the extraordinary cargo of HMS *Colossus*, which in 1798 dragged its anchors and ran onto rocks off Samson, carrying Sir William Hamilton's collection of classical Greek vases. Salvage awards could be substantial: one funded the construction in 1870 of the gig *Golden Eagle*, which is still active in gig-racing today.

Romantic tales of 'deliberate wrecking' by false lights are not supported by historical accounts and do a disservice to the islanders' many well-documented acts of heroism, putting to sea in terrible conditions to save lives, sometimes at the cost of their own. In 1907 the huge sailing vessel *Thomas W Lawson* went adrift in a gale, striking Annet and rapidly breaking up. The gig *Slippen* twice put out in rough seas seeking survivors, and two were saved by Frederick Cook Hicks who swam out into the waves. But among those lost was Hicks's father, St Agnes pilot Billy Cook Hicks, who had gone aboard the stricken vessel the previous day to advise safe passage once the gale slackened.

Thanks to its dangers, Scilly is marked by a cluster of lighthouses that embody major advances in the post-medieval development of lighthouse design. The initial request for a lighthouse to be built on St Agnes came in 1679 from the East India Company and groups

Facing page, left and right: The wreck and cargo of Cita
Above: This cast-iron cresset or firebasket from St Agnes's lighthouse, now in Tresco Abbey Gardens, may be the only one surviving in Britain
Right: The Bishop Rock Lighthouse from the east

representing London and other ports, who were fearful of losing more of their trading vessels to the rocks of Scilly. St Agnes's coal brazier was first lit in 1680 and the lighthouse was only the second to be built by the Trinity House Corporation, which runs the lighthouse service in England, Wales and the Channel Islands. Its design is an early form of the round-tower that later became dominant, but complete with gunports for defence against Dutch raiders. St Agnes's lighthouse was decommissioned in 1911 and replaced by an oil-fired light still operating on Peninnis Head, St Mary's. Perhaps most striking to modern visitors, the Bishop Rock lighthouse towers over the reefs in the west of the island group, occupying the rock on which medieval criminals were stranded, in lieu of more gory forms of execution. Initial attempts to build

a lighthouse here failed when the unfinished experimental cast-iron structure was swept away in a storm in 1850. The substantial granite tower that replaced it was first lit in 1858 and still stands. It was encased within the present lighthouse walls in 1887 after its granite blocks were found to be cracking – such are the tremendous forces that stormy seas bring to bear on this structure.

Despite modern navigational aids and its ring of lighthouses, Scilly remains no stranger to shipwrecks. The oil tanker *Torrey Canyon* achieved notoriety when it grounded on Seven Stones reef in 1967, and the grounding of the bulk carrier *Cita* in March 1997 near Porth Hellick produced scenes of shoreline salvage not witnessed since *Minnehaha*, not to mention a costly clean-up to minimise environmental impact. *Cita* slipped beneath the waves to become colonised by marine life alongside the wreck of *Lady Charlotte*, lost at the same location in 1917. She is unlikely to be the last.

Above: Castleford, *ashore off Crebawethan in 1887. The event features in Jim Crace's 1994 novel* Signals of Distress.
Facing page: St Agnes's Lighthouse

Above: The Old
Blockhouse

Facing page, left:
Looking out to sea
across the gun
platform

History

This small blockhouse was built between 1548 and 1554 to defend the harbour of Old Grimsby, on the east coast of Tresco. It formed part of a series of forts built on the islands during the reigns of Edward VI and Mary I, and followed the attempt to build a large artillery fort, known as Harry's Walls, on St Mary's.

In fact, the blockhouse did not see action until the 17th century, during the English Civil War. In 1651 a Royalist garrison was defending the islands against attack by a Parliamentarian fleet commanded by the famous Admiral Blake. Blake attacked Tresco first, capturing its fortifications without difficulty, and then used the island as a base to assault the main Royalist stronghold at Star Castle on St Mary's. Though vigorously defended, the Old Blockhouse clearly proved of little value against the longer-range guns of Blake's ships. It was replaced afterwards by the much stronger gun fort, called Cromwell's Castle, on the other side of the island, though it was still considered serviceable in the 18th century.

Description

Blockhouses are small, strongly-built defensive structures, often constructed in forward positions. Designed to house guns and protect gunners and their ammunition from attack, they were used from the late-14th to mid-17th centuries. The Old Blockhouse sits at the south-east edge of Old Grimsby harbour, from where it commands a field of fire to the north-west, across the entrance to the harbour, and to the north-east, across the waters between Tresco and Tean, one of several points of entry into the Scilly archipelago.

The simple structure here consists of a rectangular gun platform, 23 ft (7m) by 20 ft (6m), built on a natural rocky outcrop and approached by a flight of seven steps. It was once surmounted by a parapet with splayed gunports; although now partly demolished, the parapet remains up to 3 ft (1m) thick in parts. A small lean-to in the south-west corner was designed to accommodate the handful

of men charged with keeping watch. In the south wall there is a small recess which may have been an ammunition store. To the right of the entrance is a second room, with a fireplace and chimney, which was probably the later living quarters, added when the blockhouse was reoccupied during the Civil War.

The approach to the Old Blockhouse is defended by a U-shaped rampart, visible as a turf-covered bank up to 33 ft (10m) wide and 6 ft (2m) high, around the crown of the hill, while two lower ramparts survive lower down, covered in blown sand.

Above: The gun platform with lean-to shelter

On Tresco at Blockhouse Point, at S end of Old Grimsby harbour; take footpath up onto the headland
OS Map 203; ref SV 897155

This is one of the largest and best preserved of the distinctive burial chambers known as entrance graves, found mainly on the Isles of Scilly but also in west Cornwall. Dating from about 2000 BC, it is the largest such grave in a scattered cemetery that includes six other entrance graves and two low cairns.

At the time when this imposing structure was built, most of Scilly comprised a single landmass. A steady rise in sea level has since engulfed the wide central lowlands, and with them the fertile farmland that provided the economic base for the first farmers, four to five thousand years ago. As on Bodmin Moor and Dartmoor, the early farmers built their ritual monuments on the upper slopes above the cultivated land. This grave, like others on Scilly, lies close to the edge of a prehistoric field system.

Entrance graves are perhaps the most impressive of Bronze Age ritual monuments, and that at Porth Hellick Down is typical in its design. It consists of a near-circular mound, about 39 ft (12m) in diameter and up to 5 ft (1.6m) high, which is retained by a kerb of stone slabs. This mound is built around a stone-lined, roughly rectangular chamber, about 12 ft (3.5m) long and up to 5 ft (1.5m) high, which is roofed by four massive capstones. A long unroofed passage

Right: The mound over the burial chamber with its surrounding kerb

Facing page: The entrance to the chamber, almost blocked by the projecting jambstone

leads from the edge of the mound to the chamber entrance, its sides lined with stone slabs and rubble. Unusually, passage and chamber are at angles to each other rather than in line, and the junction between the two is marked by a projecting jambstone, which almost blocks the passage. Surrounding the mound is a low, circular, outer platform, about 70 ft (21m) in diameter, whose outer edge is just visible as a slight slope-break.

During the excavation of the tomb in 1899, the capstones and the kerb around the mound were exposed, as well as an outer kerb around the edge of the platform. In the course of later restoration work the platform's outer kerb was removed and the kerb around the mound was slightly modified. The chamber's contents had been destroyed or removed long before the excavation: the only finds were some fragments of Bronze Age pottery. However, entrance graves elsewhere have been found to contain cremated human bone and small burial urns – in one grave, Knackyboy Carn on

St Martin's, the remains of over 60 people were discovered. Such entrance graves remained in use over a long period, and may have performed other functions, perhaps serving as shrines or as territorial markers.

Other well-preserved entrance graves on St Mary's can be seen at Bant's Carn and Innisidgen. Related sites on the mainland include Tregiffian Burial Chamber and Ballowall Barrow.

On St Mary's, 1½ miles E of Hugh Town; signposted from Carn Friars. OS Map 203; ref SV 928108.

Six English Heritage sites in this area are staffed and most have a separate guidebook, which can be purchased at the site's gift shop or by mail order. These sites charge an admission fee, although admission is free to members of English Heritage (see inside back cover). **Please note that sites listed here as opening on 1 April open for Easter if it is earlier**. Full details of admission charges, access and opening times for all of English Heritage's sites are given in the *English Heritage Members' and Visitors' Handbook*, and on our website (www.english-heritage.org.uk).

Details of English Heritage publications can be found in the *Publications Catalogue*. To obtain a free copy of the catalogue, and to order English Heritage publications, please contact:

English Heritage Postal Sales
c/o Gillards, Trident Works
Temple Cloud, Bristol BS39 5AZ

Tel: 01761 452966 Fax: 01761 453408
email: ehsales@gillards.com

CHYSAUSTER ANCIENT VILLAGE
CORNWALL

This Celtic settlement was originally occupied almost 2,000 years ago. The 'village' consisted of eight stone-walled homesteads known as courtyard houses, which are only found on the Land's End peninsula and the Isles of Scilly. Each house had an open central courtyard surrounded by a number of thatched rooms. The houses form one of the oldest village streets in the country and are accompanied by remains of a fogou.

Open 1 Apr–31 Oct. Please call for details of admission prices and opening times: 07831 757934.

2½ miles NW of Gulval, off B3311. OS Map 203; ref SW 472350

LAUNCESTON CASTLE
CORNWALL

Launceston Castle's keep is set on the high motte of a stronghold built soon after the Norman Conquest. Beyond the motte, the castle includes a walled outer court – one of its gatehouses was famously used as a jail for George Fox during the reign of Charles II. As the venue for the county assizes and jail, the castle witnessed the trials and hangings of numerous criminals. The last execution was in 1821. A hands-on display traces 1,000 years of the castle's history, with finds from excavations.

Open 1 Apr–31 Oct. Please call for details of admission prices and opening times: 01566 772365.

In Launceston.
OS Map 201; ref SX 331846

PENDENNIS CASTLE
CORNWALL

Constructed between 1540 and 1545, Pendennis and its sister St Mawes guard the mouth of the River Fal, at the Cornish end of a chain of castles built by Henry VIII along the south coast. Pendennis has seen a great deal of active service and was continually adapted over 400 years to meet new enemies, from the French and Spanish in the 16th century through to the Second World War.

Open year-round except Christmas and New Year; Saturdays in summer may be by guided tours only. Please call for details of admission prices and opening times: 01326 316594.

On Pendennis Headland, 1 mile SE of Falmouth. Falmouth Land Train stops in the castle car park in summer.

OS Map 204; ref SW 824318

RESTORMEL CASTLE
CORNWALL

Surrounded by a deep moat and perched on a high mound, the huge circular keep of this castle, built at the turn of the 14th century, survives in good condition. Built as a symbol of wealth and status and once home to Edward, the Black Prince, it offers splendid views over the surrounding countryside. It is also a marvellous picnic spot.

Open 1 Apr–31 Oct. Please call for details of admission prices and opening times: 01208 872687.

1½ miles N of Lostwithiel, off A390. OS Map 200; ref SX 104614

ST MAWES CASTLE
CORNWALL

This most perfectly preserved of Henry VIII's coastal fortresses was built to counter the invasion threat from Europe, in partnership with Pendennis on the other side of the Fal Estuary. It fell to Parliamentarian forces in 1646 and was not properly refortified until the late 19th and early 20th centuries.

Open year-round except Christmas, New Year and some Saturdays. Please call for details of admission prices and opening times: 01326 270526.

In St Mawes on A3078.
OS Map 204; ref SW 841328

TINTAGEL CASTLE
CORNWALL

Tintagel is an awe-inspiring spot and a place of legends. Historically associated with King Arthur, a connection renewed by Tennyson in his *Idylls of the King*, Tintagel was a high status trading settlement of Celtic kings before Richard, Earl of Cornwall, built his castle there in the 13th century. The castle ruins, on the rugged windswept cliff, are breathtaking.

Open year-round except Christmas and New Year. Please call for details of admission prices and opening times: 01840 770328.

On Tintagel Head, ½ mile along uneven track from Tintagel: no vehicles. OS Map 200; ref SX 049891

CORNWALL

General

Barnatt, J *Prehistoric Cornwall: The Ceremonial Monuments.* Wellingborough: Turnstone Press, 1982

Borlase, W *Antiquities, Historical and Monumental, of the County of Cornwall…and the Scilly Islands, with a Vocabulary of the Cornu-British Language.* London: the author, 1769

Pevsner, N *The Buildings of England: Cornwall.* 2nd edn. London: Penguin, 1970

Saunders, A *Exploring England's Heritage: Devon and Cornwall.* London: HMSO, 1991

Weatherhill, C *Belerion – Ancient Sites of Land's End.* Penzance: Alison Hodge, 1981

Weatherhill, Craig *Cornovia – Ancient Sites of Cornwall and Scilly.* Tiverton: Cornwall Books, 1997

Weatherhill, C *Cornish Place Names and Language.* Wilmslow: Sigma Leisure, *c* 1995

White, P *Ancient Cornwall.* Redruth: Tor Mark Press, 2000

Ballowall Barrow

Dymond, C W *Cornwall's Ancient Stones: A Megalithic Enquiry.* Penzance: Oakmagic, 1999

Payne, R *The Romance of the Stones.* Fowey: Alexander Associates

Scarre, C (ed) *Monuments and Landscape in Atlantic Europe.* London: Routledge, 2002

Carn Euny Ancient Village

Christie, P M L *Chysauster and Carn Euny, Cornwall.* London: English Heritage, 1993

Cooke, I *Guide to Carn Euny Iron Age Village and Fogou and Other Nearby Ancient Sites.* Penzance: Men-an-Tol, *c* 1991

Dupath Well House

Meyrick, J *A Pilgrim's Guide to the Holy Wells of Cornwall.* Falmouth Printing Co, 1982

Quiller-Couch, M and L *Ancient and Holy Wells of Cornwall.* London: Charles J Clark, 1894

Whelan, E *The Magic and Mystery of Holy Wells.* Chieveley: Capall Bann, 2001

Halliggye Fogou

Cooke, I M *Mother and Sun: The Cornish Fogou.* Penzance: Men-an-Tol, 1993

Vivyan, R R, Sir, Blight, J T, and Iago, W *The Halliggye Fogou: An Ancient Cornish Earth Mystery.* Penzance: Oakmagic, 2001 (originally published Truro: Lake & Lake, 1885)

The Hurlers Stone Circles

Burl, A *The Stone Circles of Britain, Ireland and Brittany.* New Haven/London: Yale University Press, 2000

Dymond, C W *The Hurlers: Cornish Stone Circles.* Institute of Geomantic Research Occasional Papers 8, Cambridge: IGR, 1977

King Doniert's Stone

Courtney, R A *The Cornish Cross: Its Pagan Origins.* Penzance: Oakmagic, 1997

Langdon, A *Old Cornish Crosses.* Exeter: Cornwall Books, 1988

Penhallam Manor

Beresford, G *The Medieval Manor of Penhallam, Jacobstow, Cornwall.* London: Medieval Archaeology, 1954

St Breock Downs Monolith

Cooke, I *Standing Stones of the Land's End: An Enquiry into their Function.* Cornwall: Men-an-Tol, *c*1998

St Catherine's Castle

Morley, B *Henry VIII and the Development of Coastal Defence.* London: HMSO, 1976

Tregiffian Burial Chamber

Weatherhill, C *Cornovia: Ancient Sites of Cornwall and Scilly.* Tiverton: Cornwall Books, 1997

Trethevy Quoit

Borlase, W *Cromlechs and Tumuli of Cornwall.* Ceredigion: Llanerch Press, 1995

Weatherhill, C *Cornovia: Ancient Sites of Cornwall and Scilly.* Tiverton: Cornwall Books, 1997

ISLES OF SCILLY

General

Ashbee, P *Ancient Scilly.* London: David & Charles, 1974

Borlase, W *Antiquities, Historical and Monumental, of the County of Cornwall…and the Scilly Islands, with a Vocabulary of the Cornu-British Language.* London: the author, 1769

Bowley, R L *The Fortunate Islands.* St Mary's: Bowley, 1980

Ratcliffe, J *Scilly's Archaeological Heritage.* Cornwall County Council, 1992

Thomas, C *Exploration of a Drowned Landscape: Archaeology and History of the Isles of Scilly.* London: Batsford, 1985

Weatherhill, Craig *Cornovia – Ancient Sites of Cornwall and Scilly.* Tiverton: Cornwall Books, 1997

Bant's Carn Burial Chamber and Halangy Down Ancient Village

Ashbee, P 'Bant's Carn, St Mary's, Isles of Scilly: an entrance grave restored and reconsidered'. *Cornish Archaeology*, **15**, 1976, pp 11–26

Ashbee, P 'Excavations at Halangy Down, St Mary's, Isles of Scilly, 1969–70. *Cornish Archaeology*, **9**, 1970, pp 69–76

Grey, A and Ashbee, P 'Prehistoric habitation sites on the Isles of Scilly'. *Cornish Archaeology*, **11**, 1972, pp 19–49

Cromwell's Castle, Harry's Walls, Garrison Walls, King Charles's Castle and Old Blockhouse

Bowley, R L *Scilly at War.* St Mary's: Bowley, 2001

English Heritage *The Garrison, St Mary's Isles of Scilly: A Walk Around the Walls.* Leaflet available from English Heritage SW regional office

Miles, T J and Saunders, A D 'King Charles's Castle, Tresco, Scilly'. *Post-medieval Archaeology*, **4**, 1970 (1971), pp 1–30

Morley, B *Henry VIII and the Development of Coastal Defence.* London: HMSO, 1976

Saunders, A D 'Harry's Walls, St Mary's, Scilly: A New Interpretation'. *Cornish Archaeology*, **1**, 1962, pp 85–91

Spreadbury, I D *Castles in Cornwall and the Isles of Scilly.* Redruth: D Truran, 1984

Tolhurst, M *The English Civil War.* London: English Heritage, 1992

Wilkinson-Latham, R J *Discovering Artillery.* Princes Risborough: Shire, 1987

Innisidgen Lower and Upper Burial Chambers

Dimbleby, G W *A Buried Soil at Innisidgen, St Mary's, Isles of Scilly.* Redruth: Institute of Cornish Studies, 1977

Ashbee, P *Ancient Scilly: From the First Farmers to the Early Christians.* London: David & Charles, 1974

Porth Hellick Down Burial Chamber

Ratcliffe, J *Scilly's Archaeological Heritage.* Truro: Twelveheads Press, 2003

Thomas, C *Exploration of a Drowned Landscape: Archaeology and History of the Isles of Scilly.* London: Batsford, 1985

FEATURES

The Cornish Identity

Buckley, A *The Cornish Mining Industry: A Brief History.* Penryn: Tor Mark Press, 1992

Deacon, B *et al Mebyon Kernow and Cornish Nationalism.* Cardiff: Welsh Academic Press, 2003

Ellis, P B *The Story of the Cornish Language.* Penryn: Tor Mark Press, 1990

Payton, P *Cornwall: A History.* Fowey: Cornwall Editions, 2004

Stoyle, M *West Britons: Cornish Identities and the Early Modern British State.* Exeter: University of Exeter Press, 2002

Cornish Antiquarians

Michell, J A *Short Life at the Land's End. J T Blight, FSA, Artist.* Penzance: Bath Press, 1977

Pool, PAS *William Borlase.* Truro: Royal Institution of Cornwall, 1986

Thomas, C 'The fiftieth anniversary of the West Cornwall Field Club'. *Cornish Archaeology,* **24**, 1985, pp 5–14

Cornish Mining

Barton D B *A History of Copper Mining in Cornwall and Devon.* Truro: Truro Bookshop, 1961

Garrard, S *The Early British Tin Industry.* Stroud: Tempus, 2000

Stanier, P *Cornwall's Mining Heritage.* Truro: Twelveheads Press, 2002

Stovel, A and Williams, P *Images of Cornish Tin.* Ashbourne: Landmark, 2001

Timberlake, S 'Prehistoric copper mining in Britain'. *Cornish Archaeology,* **31**, 1992, pp 15–34

Todd, A C and Laws, P *The Industrial Archaeology of Cornwall.* Newton Abbot: David & Charles, 1972

Neolithic and Bronze Age Burial Monuments

Barnatt, J *Prehistoric Cornwall: The Ceremonial Monuments.* Wellingborough: Turnstone Press, 1982

Weatherhill, C *Belerion – Ancient Sites of Land's End.* Penzance: Alison Hodge, 1981

Weatherhill, Craig *Cornovia – Ancient Sites of Cornwall and Scilly.* Tiverton: Cornwall Books, 1997

Myths and Legends

Bottrell, W *Stories and Folklore of West Cornwall,* Llanerch, facsimile 1996 (1880)

Courtney, M A *Folklore and Legends of Cornwall*. Cornwall Books, 1988 (1890)

Hamilton Jenkin, A K *Cornwall and its People*. London: David & Charles, 1988 (1945)

Hunt, R *Popular Romances of the West of England*. Llanerch facsimile of 1916 edn (1990)

Weatherhill, C and Devereux, P *Myths and Legends of Cornwall*. Sigma Leisure, 1994

Writers and Artists
Brigstocke, H (ed) *Oxford Companion to Western Art*. Oxford: OUP, 2001

Chambers Biographical Dictionary. Edinburgh: Chambers, 1984

Cowan, R A *Century of Images*. London: Andre Deutsch, 1997

Cross, T *Painting the Warmth of the Sun: St Ives Artists 1939–75*. London: Lutterworth, 1996

Rowse, A L *A Cornish Childhood*. London: Jonathan Cape, 1942

Shipwrecks and Lighthouses
Fowles, J *Shipwreck* [with photography by the Gibsons of Scilly]. London: Sphere, 1981

Larn, R *Shipwrecks of the Isles of Scilly*. Nairn: Thomas & Lochar, 1993

Marriott, L *Lighthouses*. London: Parkgate Books, 1999

Noall, C *Cornish Lights and Shipwrecks including the Isles of Scilly*. Truro: D Bradford Barton, 1968

Pickwell, J *Shipwrecks around the Isles of Scilly*. St Mary's: Isles of Scilly Museum, 1980

Tarrant, Michael *Cornwall's Lighthouse Heritage*. Truro: Twelveheads Press, 1993

Useful websites relating to Cornwall and the Isles of Scilly

www.cornisharchaeology.org.uk
Cornwall Archaeological Society

www.cornwall.gov.uk
(Cornwall County Council)

www.cornwalltouristboard.co.uk
(Cornish Tourist Board)

www.cornwall-online.co.uk
(Travel, tourism, culture, history information)

www.english-heritage.org.uk
(English Heritage)

www.gibsonsofscilly.co.uk
Gibson family photography

www.scilly.gov.uk
(Council of the Isles of Scilly)

www.iosmuseum.org
(Isles of Scilly Museum)

www.nationaltrust.org.uk
(National Trust)

www.royalcornwallmuseum.org.uk
(Royal Cornwall Museum & Royal Institution of Cornwall)

English Heritage thanks the many individuals and organisations who helped to put this book together, and the communities within which these monuments are located for their continual support and assistance.

The editor would like to thank all those people within and beyond English Heritage who contributed to this book. In particular, Katy Carter who wrote the site histories and descriptions, and the authors of the special-interest features: Professor Charles Thomas for Cornish Antiquarians; Andy Norfolk for Myths and Legends; Colin Buck for Cornish Mining; Dr Bernard Deacon for Cornish Identity; Dave Hooley for Scilly Shipwrecks and Lighthouses; Dr Vince Holyoak for Neolithic and Bronze Age Burial Monuments; and Jill Sharp for Writers and Artists. Thanks also to Dave Hooley for his help throughout the project, to Derek Kendall and Charles Walker in the English Heritage photographic section, Rob Cook in the Royal Cornwall Museum library, Jacquie Meredith for proofreading, Sue Vaughan for indexing and John Goodall, Loraine Knowles and Bronwen Riley for their comments on the text.

A number of the sites in this book are in the guardianship of English Heritage but managed by other organisations, as follows: Ballowall Barrow (managed by the National Trust); Dupath Well (managed by the Cornwall Heritage Trust); Halliggye Fogou (managed by Trelowarren Estate); The Hurlers, King Doniert's Stone, St Breock Downs Monolith, Tregiffian and Trethevy Quoit (all managed by the Cornwall Heritage Trust). Management information for our paying sites, where relevant, is given in the section on pages 86–9.